THESE ARE THE TIMES . . .

by

Nelson J. Davey

VANTAGE PRESS
New York / Washington / Atlanta
Los Angeles / Chicago

A special note of thanks for their inspiration should be made to Ashby Bladen, Henry Hazlitt, Robert Rimmer, and Jude Wanniski.

FIRST EDITION

Published by Vantage Press, Inc.
516 West 34th Street, New York, New York 10001

Manufactured in the United States of America
ISBN: 533-05555-5

Library of Congress Catalog Card No.: 82-90645

Contents

Introduction
An Autobiographical Sketch

April 1955: time for a pivotal turning point in my life. This decisive event should not have been completely unexpected, for it was the predictable result of incessant thoughts, plans, and dreams since childhood.

But even so, it was an unforgettable experience, that rarest of human happenings when, for just moments, time seemed to suspend its inexorable march, while I straddle the present, reviewed the past, and reflected on plans for the future. When complete, the total experience had seemed to be more than mere physical sensation—more mystical, like some form of psychic orgasm that leaves one suffused with a lingering, satisfying glow of fulfillment.

From the very beginning it had not been the oft-quoted baser emotions like lust, envy, or greed that had driven man to cross storm-tossed seas and life-threatening virgin continents but rather his innate urge to perform positive deeds that would gain him respectful recognition from his contemporaries—deeds that when successfully completed, would leave him gorged with a feeling of accomplishment. Unquestionably, it was this quest for a sense of total satisfaction or state of grace that was in large part responsible for the drive of millions to shed the stifling attitudes of the old world in favor of the unlimited potential of the new.

Thus, like those many pursuers before me, the fire that

had started as a smoldering ember of hope, that had been fanned into a crackling fire of desire, was now a raging inferno of passion that could only be quenched by my ultimate act of accomplishment: an exodus to California.

Though I had at first wistfully hinted and then strongly urged the move, my wife, the mother of two, continued to express concern for the many potential dangers, both real and fancied, that might lie ahead.

Then one spring day, following an unusually severe winter, unexpectantly came the long hoped-for pronouncement by Barbara that she, likewise, was ready for the big challenge.

Quickly, before there could be any mind-changing, came the booking on the "El Cap" to Los Angeles; the two days and three nights of clickety-click, clickety-clack, as the train sped through the legendary land of the Old West.

Like scenes from a Saturday afternoon matinee, images of horizon-filling herds of buffalo stampeding across the plains seemed to appear through the window—only to be crowded out by visions of red-rock canyons suddenly alive with hard-riding, whooping Indians fleeing before the fast-closing, bugle-propelled cavalry.

In my whimsy even the western names seemed to ricochet across the prairie like Matt Dillon's six-guns—Dodge City, the Pecos, Santa Fe.

On the third morning, I awoke to find the train nearing the eagerly awaited depot reunion with an old friend who, earlier during work breaks in Michigan, had helped fan the California flames.

With the self-assurance of an already acclimated Californian, my friend proudly called attention to the bustling freeways, fabled Hollywood, and marrow-warming sun as we traveled out over Cahuenga Pass and on to his home in the western end of the "Valley." Off somewhere in my mind could be heard a famous Western singer's melodic invitation "to settle down and never more roam and make the San Fernando Valley my home."

Sensing that time was of the essence, early Monday morning came the job interview at Lockheed and, as though part of a script, job in hand, the decision to return to Michigan by plane that very evening.

Now the tempo of events accelerated. In quick succession came the sale of our little lakeside cottage home; the purchase of an old-but-solid two-wheeled trailer that had been constructed from the front-end of an ancient Model-A Ford; the hurried well-wishes, predictions of disaster, and tearful goodbyes from incredulous and skeptical friends, relatives, and neighbors; and, finally once again, the now week-long trek westward.

Little more than three weeks had elapsed since my wife's submissive decision, and I had crisscrossed the bulk of this continent three times—by train, plane, and auto, and now finally, as a new expectant resident, was at the long-sought destination—California!

At the very first opportunity that evening, I broke away from the resting family and reunited friends and drove a short distance further out into the valley and then on foot to a secluded, park-like clearing where, alone for the first time since our arrival, I could delight in my rising feeling of elation.

All of my senses seemed acutely attuned to this moment: my eyes observing the deepening shadows of approaching dusk; the stately palms swaying gently in the distance along Sherman Way; the vibrant colors of the oleanders, bouganvillea, and nearby Chatsworth Hills; my nose scenting the sweet aroma of orange blossoms wafting on the evening breeze; and my ears eavesdropping on the distant rumblings of civilization—sounds that only just recently had arrived to challenge the solitude of yesterday.

As I stood basking in this confluence of external awareness, my mind wandered through a montage of events from my past. In sharp focus could be seen the isolated wilds of White Fish Point, this northernmost place in Michigan to where my father had retreated with his wife and four sons in the vain hope that by teaching the area's motley band of children in the local one-room school house he could partially escape the perils of the deepening depression. The absence of other teaching and sales jobs and the resultant lack of money had forced this decision, but also, the availability of this teaching position coincided with his recent "calling" to the ministry. Though successful in achieving this latter goal, the decision had nearly proven disastrous, as the family narrowly escaped starvation when the local one-man school board decided in midwinter to replace father with an uneducated but cheaper crony.

I continued to reminisce: back to the little log church father accepted as his first ministerial assignment; to the glow of sublime faith reflected on his face as he repeatedly accepted the pitifully small "offering of his flock" secure in the knowledge that God would continue to provide; to the shared joy of the family as, five years later, we viewed the first real traditional-appearing church and parsonage assigned to father and the sudden plunge into soul-shattering despair as, just before Christmas and only days after Pearl Harbor, mother suddenly became critically ill and died; to the subsequent move to southern Michigan and the first meeting with the flirtatious twelve-year-old Barbara who would become my constant companion.

Memories continued to swirl through my head as I recalled the lasting impression made by father's one and only futile attempt at being elected Michigan Governor on the Prohibition ticket; the departure from Hastings of my father and growing new family and my decision to remain behind where now all of my personal wants and needs existed—job, school, and Barbara; my consternation, and then determination to fight, when informed by the school superintendent that I could no longer continue in high school because no one was now paying the "necessary" property tax and, the feeling of complete satisfaction when I laid guardianship papers, signed by my just-returned-from-the-Navy brother on the official's desk and returned to school; the careful hoarding of a $140 nest egg as Barbara and I impatiently awaited marriageable age—she 17, I 19; the purchase of our first small home and birth of our two children—doll-like Brenda and beautiful Gregory; and finally, the big move that has led to these moments of reverie.

Is it any wonder then, that, as I regained awareness, I became overwhelmed with the before-mentioned feeling of elation? I was young, healthy, employed, free from debt, three thousand dollars in my pocket—but most of all, we were in the promised land—California!

★ ★ ★

January 1972; time for a new, major turning-point in my life. This event, like that seventeen years earlier, was also the creation of a mind now totally comfortable in the belief that we create our own reality through direct action and that we are neither prisoners of fate nor prisoners of the past.

But the fact that previous events were not responsible for future action didn't prevent my mind from again playing its montage-like game of mental stepping-stones into the past.

The first decade in California had lived up to our expectations and had provided us with a near womb-like environment in which to raise our family.

The three thousand dollars had become the down payment on a three bedroom home in Reseda close to work, school, and shopping.

Nationally, the stable Eisenhower years were soon to be followed by the unfulfilled promises of Camelot and the Great Society. Before long the country would recognize that the seeds for future trouble were being sown with impunity. Subtle economic problems like rising inflation, unemployment, and taxes, were alternately treated with the old Keynesian economic fixes or simply ignored, while not so subtle social ills like campus unrest, racial demonstrations, and increasing crime were explained away as components of an unpopular war that would fade away as soon as the Vietnamese finally swallowed our self-prescribed dose of democracy.

By and large, however, our family had continued to busily pursue its economic and educational goals; for the most part insulated from these growing national problems.

I had quickly resumed my education at nearby Pierce College and a seemingly endless procession of semesters passed by. Increasingly, my academic interests focused on the political and economic problems that were becoming ever more apparent.

On the political scene, I became curious as to just what was meant by the term "grass-root" politics.

I soon discovered that highly motivated volunteers were a much sought-after commodity and was quickly assigned the important-sounding title of Reseda Republican Precinct Chairman. This task involved finding and coordinating the party efforts of twenty-four precinct captains. It didn't take long to come to the realization that "grass-roots" was a misnomer—it should have been more appropriately termed "asphalt or cement-roots" politics! I never walked so many miles in my life: finding workers, passing out literature, getting people registered, and finally, literally herding Republicans to the polls. Gratifyingly, the work payed off—over 90 percent voted in each of my assigned precincts.

My economic interests were accentuated by the direction my occupation had taken. Having transferred from Lockheed to North American Aviation (now Rockwell International), I eventually found myself involved in a vital, life-giving function of the company—the pricing and negotiation of major government contracts. Thus, the economy and its affect on costs had become an essential component of my daily life.

1964 found us buying a new tri-level home in nearby Simi Valley while continuing to retain the Reseda house as an investment. In addition to the increased pleasure provided by the new home, the move had been motivated by the desire to provide the best possible climate for completion of the children's high school programs.

But, in addition to the pleasure of the new home and superior schooling opportunities for the children, the move over the mountain pass provided an opportunity to expand my interest in both politics and governmental economic planning.

Simi Valley, which had been a sleepy, agricultural area for many years, away from the normal travel routes of the teeming Los Angeles basin, suddenly exploded with people; the result of new developers' interest and the completion of a new freeway that was chipped and blown through the mountain pass. It was like pulling a plug: thousands poured into Simi from the now burgeoning San Fernando Valley. Seemingly overnight, the population grew to over seventy thousand!

It soon became evident that, if the new pulsing community was to grow in a disciplined way, it would require local input into its planning. So it was that, in response to this need, a civic group was formed to incorporate the valley into a city, a task that was successfully completed in a couple of years. The project provided me with the opportunity to develop and input the essential, and what turned out to be, highly accurate financial budget forecasting data.

The spring of 1971 brought us to the close of another chapter in our life and the decision to make yet another bold move: the locating, buying, and managing of our own business. We had decided that this venture was to be recreation-oriented because statistically this was a fast growing industry. The business needed to be financially large enough to adequately support all members of the family. Both objectives were realized by the purchase of a resort in beautiful Big Sur that we aptly re-named Fernwood.

Once more came the re-enactment of that earlier exodus; this time, however, from southern California to the central coast of California. Financially, it had required much the same procedure: sale of both houses, liquidation of debts, and consolidation of funds from savings and retirement accounts. Satisfyingly, the three thousand dollars had now grown to fifty-four thousand!

Fernwood was indeed a significant undertaking. Financially, the four-hundred-thousand-dollar purchase price imposed the need for additional investors. Structurally, the resort complex consisted of several different business entities: restaurant, bar, grocery store, service station, motel, campground, and monthly rentals. These complexities demanded a business control vehicle, and, in response, a closely-held corporation was formed.

We soon learned that operating a business in a remote

rural area posed many unusual problems and, in fact, presented many outright dangers—physical as well as financial. Within the first three years we faced forest fires, floods, mud slides, road closings, gas shortages, and recessions!

But from a personal point of view, these problems and dangers, successfully hurdled, seemed only to demand more and larger challenges.

My response to these little-understood-but-incessant inner urges was to take on further expanding tasks. A personal task, for example, was to expend the time, money, and effort to become a licensed pilot. But more in keeping with this narrative, these inner feelings continued to drive me towards business expansion.

I looked in depth at several potential local ventures and even allowed my fancies to wander as far away as Florida. But, finally the expansion urge was fulfilled with the acquisition of Cambria Pine Lodge—a mere 72 miles south of Fernwood. This additional resort property provided the opportunity to further develop the managerial skills of the entire family—Brenda, her husband, and two sons going south to help manage the new venture while Greg became operations manager of Fernwood. Barbara and I soon bought a new home in Cambria and continued to float between the two busy complexes attacking problems as they arose.

Though the purchase of the additional lodge property seemed to indulge my appetite for business expansion, it didn't totally assuage my innermost personal expansion desires. This unrequited inner burning, coupled with a growing apprehension with the worsening national economic problems, led me to make a major personal committment—the writing of this book.

The research portion consisted of the reading of many thousands of pages of material and has truly been a mind-expanding process. I laid the foundation by re-reading the works of most of the great political thinkers from Plato to the present. I then read dozens of current or near-current books and articles on politics, economics, and social planning. More than a year later,

I emerged, a transformed radical liberal conservative! An impossible description? A non sequitur, you say? Then what, I ask, is a person who believes in small, highly disciplined, financially responsible government? Who believes in individual rights—economically, politically, and racially for all people? And who now is convinced it will require radical means to achieve?

In October 1980, Cambria Pines Lodge was sold. The timing was near-perfect from an investment point of view; the value had risen from a little over a million dollars to two-and-a-half million in only fifty months.

In October 1982, a gift shop "Down to Earth Gifts" was purchased in West Cambria. This acquisition was in keeping with our goal of providing money-making projects for the whole family to be involved in.

And the three thousand dollars that journeyed west with us nearly three decades ago? It had now grown to over a million!

1

The Assignment

The time is now; the place, a truly idyllic country landscape; a brilliant sun is peering down through an azure-blue, cloudless sky and bathing the grass-covered, rolling hills with its enervating warmth. A cool breeze ripples through the knee-high grass, rhythmically carrying along the sound of distant, pounding surf and gently offering a bouquet of fragrances gathered while splashing through the waves and romping through the flowers and trees.

A young man and youthful woman, hand-in-hand, approach an aged man sitting on a bluff overlooking the deep-blue, tossing sea. The older man seems deeply engrossed and oblivious to the arrival of the younger pair. The younger male reluctantly interrupts the older one's reverie: "Excuse me, sir, my friend and I are looking for Mr. Thomas Paine."

Appearing momentarily startled and somewhat irritated by the interruption, the older man hesitatingly turns and gruffly replies: "I'm Thomas Paine, what do you want of me?"

"Mr. Paine, I'd like to introduce Mary—and my name is David. We've been sent in response to your last report, to serve in whatever capacity you might deem useful; as assistants, students, or perhaps, just good listeners. As you might have expected, your warnings about the worsening world conditions are causing considerable concern upstairs."

"And well it should," Thomas Paine loudly grumbles. "I've been repeatedly reporting how things are going to hell down there and for years have been urging them to provide competent experts to advise on corrective measures—and what do they send me? A couple of damned kids!"

Before replying to the older man's curt welcome, Mary eases herself down on the grass and pulls David down beside her.

"Mr. Paine, let me just say that David and I are both pleased and extremely honored just to be sitting here at the feet of the famous Thomas Paine. From everything we've read and heard over the last several weeks, we agree completely with the general statements of confidence expressed and concur wholeheartedly with the unanimous belief that your two centuries of dedicated observation of America has uniquely prepared you for the momentous task of devising a plan that would put Americans back on the path that leads to personal fulfillment and away from the path that leads to certain destruction."

Tom Paine appears only slightly mollified by the compliments and assurance of top-level support.

"I don't need anyone to convince me of my qualifications young lady—at this moment, I'm more concerned with yours," he snaps.

"Well," responds Mary to the verbal challenge, "even though we appear young and inexperienced, it may bolster your confidence if you hear that David and I were both chosen from a large group of eager applicants for this assignment. Our selection was partially supported by the fact that we had just recently made the transition over from California. But also, the selection committee considered the fact that we were both honor students."

The older man's expression of hostility seems to waver slightly and Mary, sensing victory, hurries on.

"It may also interest you to know, Mr. Paine, that we have just completed several preparatory courses prior to coming—one of which was exclusively about your life. We've read everything in file both by you and about you; and, as I said earlier, we came away tremendously impressed by your unswerving devotion and thorough understanding of the qualities that made our late homeland the great land of opportunity that it is."

"All right, enough, enough!" interrupts Tom Paine: "There's so much to be done, we'll just have to let time and results speak for each of our capabilities."

"Fair enough," David quickly agrees. Secretly, he is relieved that the old man is letting them stay without further examination of credentials. Both he and his roommate Mary have virtually thought of nothing else but being selected for this team since their sudden departure from below.

"Mary and I both appreciate how frustrated you must be after the years of watching Americans give up, little by little, the hard-won freedoms and opportunities available at the time you left in 1809."

Now Tom Paine just can't resist this obvious invitation to reminisce. "Yes, it is frustrating to have seen man so close to complete victory over the powers of wealth and special interests and let it slip away. As you will recall, in *Common Sense* I advocated severance from England and the absurd monarchy of George the Third and in *The Crisis* I rallied the patriots through the cold winter of 1776 and to the just cause of the revolution. Then, with the outcome of the American revolution a certainty, I turned my attention and my pen to similar causes in France and in my old homeland, England. I argued—quite brilliantly I might say—in *Rights of Man* that it was time to replace the old aristocratic institutions created by the moneyed and landed elite with new, liberal institutions designed to replace the principle of privilege and heredity with new ideals based on talent and merit. Republican government, I argued, rested with the people and was intended to serve their interests alone!"

As he speaks, Tom Paine has become increasingly animate, gesturing often to emphasize a point. With a shrug of seeming resignation, he continues:

"But, alas! my great dream slowly faded. The social ferment of those years was stilled in America by a federal constitution and federalist ideology which threw the balance of political and social power back into the hands of the powerful and well-to-do."

"Well," interjects David, "you must feel there is still hope for your dream or, otherwise, why would you be willing to continue to devote all of your energies to the subject?"

"Yes, of course, there's always hope," replies Tom Paine, "but the chance of success grows dimmer with each passing moment. I am now convinced that success can only be achieved through an extensive purge of negative policies and institutions that have become increasingly more powerful, such as banks, global corporations, and insurance companies. Major improvements must also be affected in the entire legal apparatus from the judicial through the penal system—plus, rejuvenation of educational, medical, and other social institutions as well."

"Good Lord!" exclaims Mary as she bounds to her feet. "I'll say one thing, you sure don't lack for downright audacity. You must recognize that the responsible people in your planned institutional massacre represent the bulk of both money and brains in the country and won't relinquish their dominant power without a fight."

"Yes, I know," replies Tom Paine with a gesture of defiance, "but I've never been known as one who turns his back on a fight. And besides, conditions have deteriorated down there well beyond the point of Band-Aid fixes."

"Okay, but I, for one, will need a lot of convincing before I agree that such drastic measures are called for," asserts David.

"So be it," concedes Tom Paine with a shrug. "If the perceptive sage Thomas Paine can't convince the two of you as to what needs fixing down there, he deserves to fail. Now, my new young friends, what I propose is that we resume your recently interrupted education. I can promise you that before we finish we will have at least touched on your major interest irrespective of what you were studying.

"As you have undoubtedly already found out," continues Tom Paine, "we have a significant advantage in our current disembodied state over any previous learning experience you've had in that we can observe events anywhere and in any time frame we choose. This permits us to conduct our classes here in this beautiful outdoor retreat. Now, if you have no questions, let's get on to our vitally important new assignment."

"Mr. Paine, you hinted earlier that the foundation for the current deteriorating situation was laid way back when you last walked the earth. Would you elaborate on how that came about?" asks Mary.

"Yes, I agree that that's a good place to start. For the last two hundred years, Americans have been taught to revere their Constitution; and well they should, for it represented a significant improvement over any government formation document previously written. The Bill of Rights alone was an important assurance against the reappearance of the injustices the colonists had fought to eliminate. But still, the total document contained the seeds for the current debacle by establishing within it the formation of a new bureaucratic government elite that would eventually be the direct cause of today's unreasonably high taxes and excessive regulations.

"In addition, contemporary advocates of a strong federalist government, like Alexander Hamilton, were successful in founding a central banking system and in obtaining special favors such as newly available land concessions that only tended to further enrich the already wealthy.

"We'll explore these problems in greater depth shortly, but for now, let's fully understand the scope of our current assignment. The United States is facing simultaneous crises in defense, inflation, energy, productivity, and economic growth. In addition, the citizens are beset by about every kind of social disorder imaginable; disorders that in the final analysis add up to an escalating loss in self-confidence in themselves as well as in their government.

"Further, Americans have lost the cohesiveness that once was their hallmark. The social fabric is frayed by endless single-issue causes relating to such obtuse subjects as right-to-life, minority rights, or the environment; and it's not that each of these causes isn't just; it's that, while these skirmishes are being fought, the war to save and enhance the current lifestyle of Americans is being lost."

"Yes," agrees Mary. "Having just arrived from the college

campus scene, we know what you mean, Mr. Paine. But speaking of war, what really is bewildering is how the political leaders of the United States allowed the nation's military might to disintegrate so rapidly."

"Well, Mary, to see how this could happen, we first need to understand that the nation donned the mantle of superpower somewhat reluctantly. Once again the background story has its roots in the war to shake off the allegiance to the pompous King George. The fact that a small, poorly equipped band of patriots could whip the 'mighty British redcoats' lent considerable credence to the swelling belief in divine destiny and invincibility that was to grow right up until recent times.

"Further, the nation's involvement in the first two world wars of this century were reasonably justified; World War Two, in particular, being thought of as the war to make the world safe for democracy. But parenthetically, the fact that it failed to ask the world if it wanted to be saved for democracy was to lead to its first clear-cut military defeat in Vietnam. This notwithstanding, there were many justified reasons for the United States involvement in the Second World War, including its desire to protect its friends and self from the grandiose designs of the Axis powers. But most important to our present discussions was the fact that the nation arose from this conflict as the most powerful industrial and military force in the world."

"That," nods Mary, "is my point. World War Two ended only four decades ago and already America is in danger of becoming a second-rate power."

"Well, Mary, one of the inherent characteristics of democracy, which, paradoxically, is both its strength and its weakness, is the difficulty of sustaining a strong military posture. From the people's point of view, money spent for arms represents *negative* expenditure while they have need for many *positive* things. This characteristic can be dangerous, though, when their political leaders decide to play a game of showdown with a power that is not disciplined by the will of the people—as was the case when John Kennedy opted to challenge Nikita Khrushchev in the 1962 Cuban Missile Crisis. Kennedy won the showdown, but as a direct result, the Russians dedicated their energies to becoming the number one world military power—a position they have nearly attained.

"The critical issue now is whether the arms race isn't jeopardizing the continued existence of the human race on the planet. The statistics would indicate that as the two superpowers jockey for supremacy, a degree of total irresponsibility, bordering on madness, has set in. There now exists, for example, the equivalent of a *ton* of TNT in nuclear power for every man, woman, and child on earth! Equally unbelievable is that, in a world that sees millions starving to death, the major powers somehow justify the expenditure of a billion dollars a day to kill and maim!"

"Yes, Mr. Paine, we understand your frustration and anger. But what can be done to restore sanity to the arms race?" asks Mary.

"The first step is to get the political leaders from both sides to start making sense in their policies and pronouncements and stop reacting to the desires of the military establishment in their country. For example, the position of the current Republican administration, discouraging resumption of the SALT talks until the United States achieves military superiority over the Russians, is sheer hypocrisy. The process of de-escalation is completely dependent on convincing rational men who understand the existing potential for mass extinction to sit and negotiate their country's security requirements. With applied diligence, those discussions could define successive lower plateaus of weapon equivalancy that could then be both achieved and verified.

"On a related subject, the United States must unilaterally cease arming the world. Far too often the sale of munitions to one country is soon followed by similar sales to its neighbors. There simply is no rationale that can further justify this course of action—not more jobs and definitely not more profit!"

"Hear, Hear!" shout Mary and David in unison. "As you can readily see, we both agree completely. But forgive me if I remind you of the many persons that have advocated similar plans for weapon reduction—but to no avail."

"Yes, David, you're quite correct in your pessimistic assessment of the past. I can only ask that you withhold further judgment as to the possibility of future success in this area until we have agreed on a comprehensive plan for attacking all of the current crises. I am convinced they are all interrelated."

"Okay, that sounds fair enough. Where do we go from here?" asks Mary.

2

Money, Inflation, and the Federal Reserve

With the look and stance of an experienced professor, Thomas Paine continues:

"Now I don't want either of you to feel that I'm being in any way condescending with my elemental approach to the material we're about to cover; its just that it is essential that we share a mutual understanding of the various economic concepts currently in vogue before we attempt to devise solutions to the nation's serious economic problems.

"First, then, I would like to briefly outline the origins of money. Initially, the desire or need for goods or services that individuals lacked was satisfied by a system known as barter. One simply swapped something owned and unneeded, for something someone else owned and no longer needed. All that was necessary for completing a transaction was an understanding and acceptance of the relative value of the two items being exchanged—one role of fine cloth for one unsheared sheep, for example.

"But before long it became necessary to make transactions less cumbersome. A substitute for the real merchandise was needed to facilitate trading where items or services were needed, but needed at a future time. The qualifications for this substitute required that it be transportable, thus, be reasonably small and light; that it retain a fairly stable exchange value; and most importantly, that it be acceptable for exchange by both parties to the transaction.

"Initially, various relatively scarce items, such as precious stones or rare materials, were used to meet these qualifications; but hassles continued to arise over an agreed value by size and grade. This deficiency was ingeniously removed when someone struck on the idea of minting coin from pure gold or silver. This would have been a perfect solution if greedy traders and, ultimately, unscrupulous governments, hadn't discovered that additional coins could be made from the original by debasing the mineral content or by shaving down the size—an illusory trick known as 'clipping.'

"As an interesting aside, every one of the modern monetary units originated as units of weight of either gold or silver. Thus, the British unit, the 'pound sterling,' is so named because it originally meant simply 'one pound of silver.' You can see how destructive inflation has been to this unit of money when you realize that the pound sterling is now worth slightly more than one-sixth of an *ounce* of silver. Even more pertinent to our assignment is that the 'dollar' was originally a Bohemian coin consisting of an ounce of silver—later redefined as 1/20, then 1/35 of an ounce of gold. Here, likewise, inflation has shrunk the value of the current dollar to slightly less than one four-hundredth of an ounce of gold!

"A more recent step in the creation of today's currency exchange system occurred when it became evident that certain men could be trusted to store valuable merchandise, particularly gold or silver. In exchange for the minerals, the storeman gave a receipt that in time came to be recognized as an acceptable substitute for the real merchandise in trade transactions. Thus today's currency, checks, or other financial paper had its origin as a simple warehouse receipt."

Hands clasped behind his back, the white-haired master paces back and forth as he continues to speak:

"Many of your contemporaries are suspicious, and not without justification, that the real culprit lurking behind many of the current social and economic disorders is money. So, let me ask you Mary, what immediate thought comes to mind when you think of the word 'money'?"

"Well," replies Mary with a sly grin, "I know I never had enough of the stuff when I needed it—and what little I did have seemed to buy less and less."

"All right; and did anyone have an explanation for why your money was buying less and less?" further queries Tom Paine.

"Yes, most everyone blamed it on inflation."

"And, unquestionably, their assessment was correct," agrees Tom Paine. "Except, few understand the full range of this economic thievery. Inflation negatively affects virtually everyone and everything it comes in contact with. As you found out Mary, it seriously degrades the value of money. But, further, it systematically destroys past and present savings—and thus, discourages further thrift; it lowers most everyone's standard of living; it imposes what is, in effect, a tax that widens the financial gap between the haves and have-nots; it corrupts both private and public morals; and it generally undermines confidence in the nation's political and economic system."

"Lordy!" exclaims David, "I knew inflation was bad news but I didn't realize it affected that many facets of people's lives."

"Yes, and the truly ironic part is that both the definition and the parties responsible for inflation are known," continues Tom Paine with a renewed look of determination.

"Unbelievable!" gasps Mary. "With the knowledge of what it is and who causes it, why is inflation permitted to exist?"

"When we arrive at the answer to that question, Mary, we shall have made significant strides towards developing our solution to inflation," answers Tom Paine.

"Let's start with an almost universally accepted definition: *Inflation is an increase in the volume of money and bank credit in relation to the volume of goods*. Do these nineteen words suggest anything to either of you?"

"Well," David thoughtfully answers, "it could suggest what appears to be an all-too-obvious answer—stop increasing money and credit, and inflation should stop."

". . . Or," adds Mary, "it could also suggest that an increase in goods in relation to the existing supply of money and credit could also stop inflation."

"Good! Both deductions are correct—at least in theory. Now, as you may have guessed, there are numerous misunderstandings prevailing in relation to this subject. For example, confusion reigns because many refuse to restrict the use of the word 'inflation' to mean an increase in the volume of money or credit; but, instead use the word to mean 'a rise in prices.' The problem here is that this latter usage confuses the disease for its symptoms.

"But in an even more elemental way, there is both misunderstanding and lack of understanding concerning the subject of money in general. For example, few understand how money or credit is created in the first place—much less how it is increased to cause inflation. Does either of you know how this process works?"

"Well, Mr. Paine," offers David, "I can remember enough of Econ. 101 to know that sophisticated governments no longer simply crank up the ol' printing press when they want to pay for goods and services they don't have money to pay for."

"Right. That's because they have evolved a far more sophisticated system to achieve their goal. The system has even been given fancy titles like 'monetary expansion' or 'monetary policy' and is implemented in America by the Federal Reserve."

"Question," interrupts Mary. "Are the two terms 'inflation' and 'monetary expansion' synonymous?"

"No, no!" emphatically replies Tom Paine. "As you will see, as we examine four critical events of this century, inflation is the intentional consequence of monetary expansion.

"The first critical event was the creation of the Federal Reserve System in December of 1913. The 'Fed,' as it was quickly dubbed, was given a legislative mandate to pursue monetary policies designed to—get this—foster stable economic growth and prevent recurrence of the frequent recessions that had been endemic over the previous century. Inflation, ironically, had not been particularly a problem during this period because the government was unable to create money beyond the needs of the people. There was a built-in monetary governor: people, local or international, could, at will, trade twenty dollars in paper for an ounce of gold.

"Prior to the start of the twentieth century then, the dollar was literally as good as gold; and as long as this remained true, people had an easy way of controlling inflation: when confidence was shaken in the dollar, they simply redeemed their paper for gold at the Treasury. Due to its relative scarcity, the real value of gold, of course, had remained quite stable.

"However, the bankers, with the support of the politicians, did not want this constraint on the volume of money to exist; so, they designed a system that reduced popular control over the money supply.

"The economy, of course, runs on money. So, it seemed obvious that control over the amount of it, either in the form of cash or credit, would essentially influence how the economy would perform.

"In addition to the relatively simple task of supplying coin and currency to its member banks, the Fed was given several other highly influential monetary powers. First, it was authorized to set the amount of reserves the member banks would be required to keep in the regional bank as back-up to their checking and savings accounts. Previously, most banks had been required to retain a reserve of twenty-five percent of total deposits in cash in the bank's own vaults. Through the Federal Reserve Act, the reserve requirements were reduced to as little as twelve percent for checking accounts and five percent on savings accounts. Because these reserves had not previously been available for loans, the reduction in size of the reserve requirement had the affect of increasing the amount of credit available to borrowers, thus increasing the bank's profits.

"A second important power assigned the Fed was the control of the discount rate, the interest rate charged on funds member banks would be permitted to borrow from the Fed. Think about this power this way: if it cost the bank more money to borrow their funds they would naturally pass this additional expense on to their customers in the form of higher interest rates for loans—and these higher rates would then have a significant affect in dampening economic activity.

"A third power made available to the Fed was control over the interest rate ceilings permitted on savings accounts. An increase in this rate, it was thought, would encourage customers to increase their savings and thus make more money available for the banks to loan.

"Also, with the creation of the Federal Reserve System came the introduction of a new kind of currency in America—the Federal Reserve Note. Unlike the existing money, this money was not redeemable in gold or silver; it was merely an IOU issued by the banks as an instrument of debt. The Federal Reserve Act only required that these notes by redeemable in lawful money on demand.

"Freed from the requirement of redeeming all paper money for gold and silver, the Fed was now able to back its notes with debt. The policitians also favored this, because, in practice, much of the money printed by the banking system went to finance Federal budget deficits.

"But the most powerful tool of all was the power to intervene directly in the financial markets via its open market operation. On paper at least, the plan was brilliant. The officials of the Federal Reserve would attempt to continually monitor and adjust the level of bank reserves they believed necessary to meet the economy's current money needs. When these reserves rose or fell above this optimum level, they were to authorize the purchase or sale of U.S. Treasury securities. These transactions, handled through the Federal Reserve Bank of New York, were bound to have an immediate and dramatic affect on the amount of money left in the total system at any time.

"For example, the New York Fed would pay for securities it wanted to purchase by depositing a check, drawn on thin air, in the seller's bank account, thus adding to the amount of money available for lending. In reverse, when the Fed wanted to sell securities, money would be transferred out of the bank, thus reducing the amount of money in the banking system.

"The trouble is, as sophisticated as the Federal Reserve system has become, it has failed in its primary duties—the control of inflation and elimination of recessions!

"Partly, this failure is due to the fact that relatively small money transactions by the Fed have a magnified effect on the economy as a whole. To illustrate this effect, let's suppose the New York Fed decides to buy one hundred thousand dollars in Treasury bills. To pay for these securities, the Fed writes a check on itself that is deposited in a member bank which now has one hundred thousand dollars of new resources. If the bank is required to hold say, ten percent, or ten thousand dollars in reserve, it can then lend the remaining ninety thousand dollars. The borrower, a local businessman, can then deposit this money in a second bank boosting the money supply again, this time by ninety thousand dollars. This process can continue until all of the original one hundred thousand dollars from the Fed is held as reserve to back up new accounts. At this point, the money supply may have expanded by as much as a million dollars!

"The important point to be remembered here is that similar expansion occurs whenever money from any source is deposited in a bank, or most recently and significantly, a savings and loan association, that then makes these deposits available for loans. Obviously, this expansion process greatly magnifies the control task assigned to the Federal Reserve.

"Another reason the Fed has failed its primary duties, is that the composition of the economy continues to change, with major monetary segments escaping beyond the Fed's control. Primarily, the one power remaining is its control over member bank reserves—and this power grows weaker as more and more members become increasingly disenchanted with the Fed and leave the system.

"Recently, as a result of major increases in interest rates, a mass exodus of capital from insurance policies to more lucrative investment opportunities occurred, once again significantly affecting this previously available source of investment capital.

"Perhaps the largest segment of the money supply to flee the Feds control is the approximate half *trillion* dollars that now lies in the hands of foreign investors. This segment is particularily troublesome because it is largely undisciplined and its size is such that it can—and does—influence investment decisions in all markets, including commodity, stocks and bonds, and private and commerical real estate.

"The failure of the Fed to satisfactorily perform is not solely their fault, however. Congress, in concert with recommendations from recent administrations, continues to apply fiscal policies that discourage investment and saving. The near-confiscatory level of taxation now in effect has endless repercussions throughout the economy. We will return to fiscal policy and taxation later, but most pertinent to this discussion is the effect such tax policy has on capital investment.

"Finally, perhaps the most important reason the system has failed to halt inflation, is that many politicians, in harmony with Fed officials just plain don't want it to stop! Mostly this is due to a misplaced belief that some expansion of the money supply creates a good business climate and is therefore good economics and good politics. Parenthetically, the present goal is for the Fed to control the annual increase in money supply to between three and-a-half and six percent—and we've just seen what affect that goal can have.

"But also, there are, and have been, political leaders such as Lyndon Johnson who deliberately used inflation to pay for foreign adventures by running up the national debt and subsequently requiring that the expenditures be repaid with cheapened dollars.

"I don't want to leave the impression, however, that deficit spending by the government is always or necessarily inflationary. It's only true when the government—the administration, Congress and the Fed—decides to intentionally inflate the money supply as a means of paying the resultant debt. One alternative previously employed was the sale of government bonds. This method, used extensively to finance World War II, for example, had the affect of postponing demand until a time when adequate supply of merchandise became available.

"My, my—I see some blank stares," reflects Tom Paine as he pauses.

"Well, I follow how money expands in the Federal Reserve System," offers David, "and I think I understand why the Fed has not been a resounding success. But I'm having trouble mentally relating all of this big picture to how it affects the ordinary citizen down there."

"The current two-hundred-billion projected annual deficits are particularily worrisome because they invite inflationary actions and because the resultant borrowing by the government will ultimately compete with the private sector's need for additional capital—thus, forcing interest rates higher and halting the current economic recovery."

3

Critical Monetary Events and Productivity

"All right, David; let me take a step further back and elaborate," responds Tom Paine with a nod of resignation. "We know that a relatively small portion of the total dollar volume of trade transactions in the economy is accomplished via hand-to-hand currency payments—most being paid with checks drawn against bank deposits. It should be self-evident that nothing in this elementary economic cycle can be inflationary in itself; similar to our earlier acquaintance, the barter system, people are simply exchanging a check for goods or services rendered. But, as we now know, it is when the quantity of money in relation to the quantity of goods increases, that the distortion called inflation arises.

"Once again, it should now stand to reason that if the supply of goods doesn't increase at approximately the same rate as the supply of money, the price of the goods will go up. Or, to put it differently, each dollar becomes less valuable because there are more dollars available to be offered for a particular item then before the expansion took place. The price, then, is simply the negotiated exchange rate or value of goods or services as expressed in a monetary unit such as the dollar.

"Let's reinforce this concept by relating to our earlier barter example—one roll of fine cloth for one unsheared sheep. If a ship arrived with a new cargo of fine cloth, the merchant-owner might be willing to trade *two* rolls of fine cloth for *one* unsheared sheep. Or, on the other hand, if when the sheepherders drove the flocks down from the high grazing country, it was discovered that the ewes had dropped an unusually abundant number of lambs, the sheep-owner might very well decide to exchange *two* sheep for *one* roll of fine cloth. The deciding variable in either exchange being, of course, an increase in quantity—both traders, finding they possessed an abundance of their product, then placing a smaller value on each unit.

"Also note, in the two hypothetical examples used here, only one of the two commodities offered for trade changed in value. We'll concede that it's perfectly possible that both could, of course; and both could even return to a new equity position of two cloth for two sheep; but for the moment, I simply want to note the fact that there was no change in the intrinsic value of the product that hadn't changed in quantity.

"Now, you'll recall," continues the ol' teacher, "that an important step in the evolution of money occurred when a substitute for one of the products in the transaction was introduced. What was being sought was a commodity that would have a relatively stable value—that could be used like a gauge to evaluate the relative worth of the various products being offered in the marketplace.

"Two things ultimately happened to diminish the usefulness of the resultant product, money, as a gauge, however.

"First, the real value of the original form of money, coins, was largely destroyed by debasing the mineral content or size. Second, when money had evolved to currency and other financial paper from a warehouse receipt for stored minerals, the new warehouseman, government, unscrupulously issued as many receipts, now called dollars in the U.S., as they saw fit; ignoring, in effect, the quantity of material the receipt was intended to represent!

"Thus, money now fails its primary role as a gauge of relative value in the marketplace because its volume is no longer predictable and because it is no longer believable as a receipt for nonexistent merchandise, gold.

"When people obtain more of anything, including money,

they value it less. Generally, therefore, goods rise in price not because there are fewer items available for sale, but because there are more dollars available to offer for them and they are, therefore, valued less.

"But I don't want to leave the impression that a rise in price can only result from an increase in money—it can indeed also result from a shortage in goods. The price of corn, for example, may go up either due to a decrease in supply caused by a crop failure or because money has increased due to inflation.

"Now, hopefully that elaboration of elementary economics will help ease your confusion, David; but if not, don't despair, for we will continue to explore all aspects of this subject until we each feel completely conversant with it.

"At this point, then, I'd like to retrogress slightly and cover some of the economic events that followed the passage of the Federal Reserve Act in 1913.

"As quickly as they could, the bankers started utilizing their new monetary system. They embarked on a program of cash and credit expansion aided by the additional need to finance the debt arising out of the First World War. With bank reserve requirements sharply reduced, the banks greatly expanded credit. By the middle of 1930, they had more than doubled the volume in savings and checking accounts that existed prior to entry into the war.

"More than one hundred and fifty years earlier I had written: 'One of the evils of paper money is that it turns the whole country into stock jobbers. The precariousness of its value and the uncertainty of its fate continually operate, day and night, to produce this destructive effect.' The subsequent boom of the twenties and bust of the thirties underscored the truth of my maxim. People of all classes mortgaged their souls to buy stocks hoping to find a shortcut to the easy life.

"Then came the big bust, and as the depression gained momentum, many bankers argued that more 'flexibility' was needed in the monetary system. To this end, a legal tender law was enacted in 1933 which had the effect of taking the country off the gold standard. Only foreign governments could still convert their dollars to gold. This act gave the bankers and politicians complete freedom to increase the volume of money and credit to any amount they chose. Since then, literally hundreds of billions of uncollateralized paper dollars have been printed.

"The third critical monetary event occurred in 1944 when representatives of the Western countries met in Bretton Woods, New Hampshire to establish a new international monetary structure. The new system established the U.S. dollar as an international reserve currency in settlement for all international debts. All other currencies in the system were pegged at fixed exchange rates against the dollar. The dollar, in return, was guaranteed by the U.S. government to be worth one thirty-fifth of an ounce of gold. But significantly, foreign central banks retained their right to trade in their dollars in exchange for gold at any time.

"As the smoke of the Second World War cleared, the American economy emerged as far and away the strongest in the world and this condition allowed the United States to help its allies and conquered foes in rebuilding. But also, it allowed the U.S. to use its newfound status of the dollar as an international reserve currency to cover the printing of vast sums of money. By artificially pegging the dollar exchange rate to prewar levels, the foreign governments were encouraged to obtain dollars to hold as reserves and with which they could conduct trade.

"By the sixties, it became increasingly obvious that devaluation of the dollar was inevitable. The quantity of dollars had increased and the amount of gold had decreased to the point that conversion at thirty-five dollars per ounce was no longer possible. Finally, in August of 1971, Richard Nixon officially repudiated the promise of the U.S. Government to back the dollar with gold.

"In effect, the government had threatened bankruptcy when it closed the gold window. It is no mere coincidence that this tossing-off of the last vestige of gold restraint upon the governments of the world was followed by the double-digit inflation of 1973 and 1974; and, by similar inflation in the rest of the world.

"Think of it this way; the gold in Fort Knox belonged no more exclusively to the government than the minerals that were being held by our old friend the warehouseman of years gone by. Imagine the result if, upon returning to the warehouse and presenting his receipt for his gold or silver, our ancient depositor had been told that the warehouseman had decided to keep the stored minerals but not to be concerned, however, because he could still use the receipt for trading purposes!

"Now, getting on with concepts that are considered causes of inflation, let's briefly explore the so-called wage-price spiral. This monetary perception contends that increases in wages will cause an increase in the price of goods, which will cause another increase in wages, and so on, in a continual upward spiral—and, that this spiral is a major cause of inflation. To understand what really happens with excessive wage demands requires that we gain greater insight into the make-up of the economy as a whole and into the subject of productivity.

"Let me ask either of you how you'd expect prices to react in relation to time if there were no outside interference?" queries Tom Paine.

"I have a suspicion that, even though I rarely saw it happen, prices would generally fall if left alone," guesses Mary.

"Yes, and your suspicion would be correct. In fact, throughout most of the nineteenth century and first half of the twentieth century, except for war periods, prices fell; and yet the economy was growing and industrializing. Historically, *falling prices are the normal function of a growing market economy.*

"Now, let's assume for the moment that we're a manufacturer who decides to market a new electric coffee pot. The first thing we would do is to conduct a market analysis to determine the degree of competition and to establish the potential demand for our new product. From this analytical data an initial production quantity would be determined, along with plans as to how to best fit this additional production into existing facilities.

"Among other considerations, the manufacturing production plan would require us to determine how automated or labor-intensive the production run should be. When this relationship had been decided, a time and motion study would then be conducted to determine, in conjunction with data from previous similar operations, the quantity of labor hours required to produce each of the first units. This data, expressed in hours and minutes, would then be plotted on a graph that is then termed a 'learning curve.' The graph, or learning curve, might indicate, for example, that it will take five hours and ten minutes of labor to produce the first unit but only two hours and thirty-five minutes to produce the thousandth unit. This drop in labor requirements over time is called *productivity*.

"When these hours are converted to labor dollars and added to material and overhead estimates, a fairly reliable approximation of the total production *cost* at various points in the production run can be made. The *price*, however, may initially bear little resemblance to the cost because it must consider the *average* production cost plus a *profit*. Frequently, to meet the competiveness of the marketplace, the early production units will be sold below cost.

"Let me digress for a moment and comment on the subject of profit. A favorite hypothesis of inflation is that greedy businessmen persist in arbitrarily marking up prices in order to increase their profits. The adherents to this conjecture should be curious enough to ask why businessmen are more greedy since World War Two than in the previous nearly inflation-free one hundred and fifty years; or why, if these unscrupulous businessmen are in the position to increase prices at will, they stop with only a paltry ten or fifteen percent increase. Of course, as we have just learned, inflation is caused by deliberate government action and not by businessmen—greedy or otherwise.

"There are several points that I want to make regarding our brief encounter with the manufacturing process. First, as it relates to productivity, it is the result of a wide array of causes, both of human and mechanical origin.

"On the human side are labor savings resulting from improved planning, more efficient use of time in various operations, and better working conditions, to name but a few. On the mechanical side, improvements in machines and tooling, and changes in automated techniques can materially reduce the quantity of hours and thus increase productivity. In addition, I want to note that any of the above factors plus numerous others, including one very important consideration—age and condition of plant and equipment—can also influence productivity. Indeed, it is the degradation of plant and equipment in American industry in recent years that has become one of the principle causes of decreasing productivity.

"Most germaine to our assignment, though, is how productivity relates to the wage-price spiral and to inflation. So, David, let me ask you this: What would happen if our employees in our mythical manufacturing plant demanded and got a wage increase *less* than the gain evidenced by productivity?"

"If I've followed your trend of thought," replies David, "the answer, at least in the short run, is nothing. I suspect in the long run, though, it might eventually affect our competitive position."

"Good. Now Mary, let me ask you what the result would be if our workers were given a wage increase *larger* than the productivity indicated by our production," continues Tom Paine.

"Well, Mr. Paine, I anticipated your question; but I'm caught in a mental quandary. The question invites the answer that such an increase would be inflationary. But that answer violates your caveat earlier that warned against using an increase in price as a definition of inflation."

"Excellent. Your answers assure me that you are really paying attention," compliments Tom Paine. "The correct answer is that *unemployment,* not inflation would be the result of excessive wage demands. That portion of the increased labor cost that exceeded productivity would have to be reflected by an increase in the price of our coffee pots, for example, and this would eventually decrease the demand for them. We would thus need fewer people to produce fewer items. Result—unemployment.

"The present economy in the United States is divided into roughly three equal sectors: private manufacturing, private services, and public services. The example just given relates to the manufacturing sector only.

"Now, an inherent characteristic of productivity is that it relates to decreases in time required to produce goods.

"For the most part, though, speed is not an essential characteristic of services. Other distinctions, such as quality, are the prime consideration in services concerned with directing traffic, repairing a damaged heart, or waiting on a table of diners, for example. By and large, then, productivity is a nonexistent element as it relates to the second and third sectors of the economy named earlier—private services and public services. And herein lies a little understood problem; increasingly, services employees demand pay increases comparable to increases received in the manufacturing sector. But without productivity to absorb part or all of the increased cost, one of two unfortunate conditions results: in the private services sector, the result is the same as in the private manufacturing sector—unemployment; in the public services sector, because it is generally insensitive to layoffs, unwarranted increases simply cause *increased taxation*.

"We've now explored the chronic and vacillating inflation in contemporary America: the unfortunate product of a continuing shift in this century from gold-backed money to government-issued paper as the standard money; and of development of central banking legislatively empowered to create money and credit from thin air. But we have not yet examined the relation these events have to the problems of business cycles or recessions."

4

The Business Cycle, Recessions, and Taxes

"The business cycle arrived in America about the time I arrived from England," continues Tom Paine. "It was unprecedented, but soon became a regularly recurring series of booms and busts; of inflationary periods marked by increased business activity, higher employment and higher prices followed by recessions or depressions marked by declining business activity, higher unemployment, and price declines, recovery, and repeat of the cycle.

"Initially, there were no explanations for the cyclic condition. There had been ups and downs in business activity before the late eighteenth century, of course; but the cause had been readily discernible: famine, wars, or an occasional overthrow of a monarch. But with the exception of these one-time events, the free market had operated rather smoothly and efficiently.

"It soon became evident that the phenomenon only occurred in the most economically advanced areas or the more advanced countries and was coincident with the growth of industrialization and commercial banking.

"By the nineteenth century, two theories had begun to emerge to explain the new and unwelcome cycles; one, by those blaming it on the growth of industry and the other, by those centering the blame on the banking system. Among the economists who centered on the market were those who, like Karl

Marx, called for abolition of the free market system and those who, like the more recent John Maynard Keynes, advocated strict government regulation. On the other hand, some economists placed the blame outside the market economy and developed the monetary theory of the business cycle.

"David Ricardo, the father of the latter school, held that the banks, spurred on and controlled by the government and its central bank, were responsible and started the cycle by expanding credit. As credit expanded, the money supply would expand. The expansion of the money supply would raise prices and set the inflationary boom into motion. Soon domestic prices would increase more rapidly than imported prices and cause imports to increase and exports to decrease—and as a result, cause a deficit in the balance of payments.

"Until recently, this imbalance assured that gold would flow out of the inflating country to pay for the additional imported merchandise. But as gold flowed out, the expanding money and banking pyramid became increasingly top-heavy, and the banks found themselves in financial danger. To save themselves, the banks then found it necessary to stop their expansion and to quickly contract their bank loans and checkbook money. The sudden shift from credit expansion to contraction reversed the economic picture and bust quickly followed boom.

"This monetary theory of business cycles had several notable features. It accounted for the behavior of prices by focusing on changes in the supply of bank money which always increased during booms and decreased during busts. It also accounted for the behavior of the balance of payments. But most importantly, it linked the boom and the bust, so that the bust was seen as the natural consequence of the boom. In short, the bust was properly shown as what it was, and not as a visitation from hell or 'the ethereal result of the inner workings of the mystical market economy.' "

Tom Paine has again been pacing back and forth, hands clasped behind his back as he continues his dissertation. He pauses momentarily and David, seizing upon the hesitation, interrupts with a question.

"Mr. Paine, your explanation of the monetary theory of booms and busts is very informative and, for the most part, dovetails nicely with your previous explanations of money, credit, and the Federal Reserve System. But one statement seems to be contradictory. You just said that at one point in the business cycle, gold flowed out of the inflating country to pay for the imbalance existing between imports and exports. But, as we now know, since Richard Nixon closed the gold window in 1971, gold has ceased being a necessary component to international trade transactions."

"Yes, David," nods Tom Paine as he returns to his pacing. "But remember I prefaced my statement with 'until recently.' As we will see, the current alternative to the outflow of gold is also troublesome.

"We now know that a new monetary world has arrived as a result of several critical economic events that occurred in the twentieth century, starting with the creation of the Federal Reserve System in 1913.

"With the gold standard eliminated as a result of the several actions explained earlier, it encouraged the Fed to increase the money supply all the time, whether it be boom or recession. In fact, there hasn't been a contraction of the money supply since the early 1930s and, what's more, there is not likely to be one until new constraints on banking activity can be devised and implemented."

"Boy, we're sure building a powerful case against the Federal Reserve System," interjects Mary.

"The truth is, Mary, the Fed has done a pretty good job of building such a case on its own. Our current task lies largely in recognition of cause-and-effect events and ultimately in devising a sane alternate plan," cautions Tom Paine. "But before we get ahead of ourselves, let me give you a few additional thoughts on the subject of recessions.

"In the old classic recession, consumer goods prices were always going up relative to capital goods—those machines or materials used to produce other goods. Even as consumer goods prices might fall by, say, ten percent in a particular recession, capital goods prices might fall by perhaps thirty percent; thus, consumer prices were rising substantially in relative terms. But from the point of view of the consumer, the fall in the cost of living was welcome, and indeed was the only sugar-coating on the bitter pill of recession or depression. Even in the depression of the 1930s, those who were lucky enough to have a job still enjoyed relatively bargain prices for consumer goods.

"But now, even the sugar-coating has been removed from the pill. Now that the supply of money—thus general prices—is never allowed to fall, the rise in relative consumer goods prices during recessions is reflcted as a rise in nominal prices as well. The cost of living now goes up even in recessions and so the poor consumer now gets the worst of both worlds. At least, before the days of government interference, he only had to suffer one calamity, like unemployment, at a time."

"It would appear that we've come back to the same culprit in this discussion as before—government," suggests Mary as she shakes her head.

"Yes, we should now see that each of these economic problems emanates from the same source," agrees Tom Paine. "Inflation, recessions, unemployment, high interest rates all have their origin in the government's decision to expand the supply of money and credit. But to add to this admittedly bad situation, the government further exacerbates these problems by trying to balance the application of its unwise monetary policy by employing both sides of an equally unwise fiscal policy—deficit government spending and excessive taxation.

"The economic effect of government spending depends on what the spending is for as compared with what the private spending it displaces would have been for. Obviously, there are some goods and services that the government can supply best; and to the extent that taxes are used for essential police, roads, or sewers, they are justified. But government spending, even on necessary goods or services, can quickly become excessive; and because excessive spending, whether for necessary or unnecessary programs or waste, reduces consumer production, it is potentially an economic evil.

"Some forms of taxation are worse than others. Perhaps the worst is heavy taxing of corporate earnings because it discourages business and productive output, reduces employment, and prevents capital formation, which is vital to the health of all business. Even so-called 'progressive income tax' is damaging to incentives and capital formation when applied in excess.

"The higher any tax gets the greater damage it does. It cannot be emphasized too strongly—the higher the level of government spending, the higher the level of taxation—and the higher the level of taxation, the more it discourages, distorts, and disrupts production!

"Mary, you have been periodically calling our attention to the case that has been building against the federal government. I'm sure it will interest you to know that there is a recently-arrived, formidable opponent of the present form of government ready to eliminate it!

"In fact, this opponent of the present form of government claims that not only has the nation-state outlived its usefulness, but only it is now capable of taking over the task of providing for man's peaceful well-being. If I add that the nation-state's recent admitted enemy is also an avowed enemy of communism and socialism, can either of you guess who or what it might be?" tantalizes Tom Paine.

5

The Nation-state vs. the Global Corporation

"Wow!" exclaims Mary. "That's a fascinating mind-teaser, Mr. Paine. Who or what recently-arrived something believes governments to be expendable and is neither communist nor socialist? Is that the question?"

"Well, you've reshaped the question somewhat, but let me supply some additional background information and see if the identity of our mystery protagonist doesn't become evident.

"As we've been discovering in our discussions, the failures and inadequacies of the nation-state are becoming increasingly obvious. Now even the most powerful capitalist nation isn't able to defend its borders from nuclear attack or solve its many internal problems of inflation, unemployment, or urban decay. But these deficiencies aren't restricted solely to capitalist states; socialism, too, is proving impotent when challenged with similar problems. Despite the seemingly recent advances of communism as an ideology in some parts of the world, it is running out of steam. Unquestionably, the countries of Eastern Europe, including the Soviet Union, appear more and more to share the capitalist goals of economic growth and consumer abundance.

"Rising out of the ashes of shared failures, though, a new force has arisen in less than a generation to challenge all other ideologies for supremacy—the global corporation! But despite the ups and downs of the Cold War, the disappointments of state socialism and capitalism, global corporations have yet to achieve the legitimacy they are seeking. Indeed, the growth of suspicion and hostility toward large business enterprises has virtually matched the growth of their power.

"The development of international production and the world market was an attempt to revitalize an economic system which in the 1930s appeared headed for catastrophe. By this time, many companies had attained near-monopoly status within their field and, because the first law of near-monopoly—or, as the economists call it, oligopoly—capitalism is growth, many of these great firms had outgrown national markets.

"But trade rivalries with other countries hampered the growth of the wider market and contributed to the financial pressures that resulted in World War II. After the war, great areas of the earth—Russia, Eastern Europe, China—passed under various forms of state socialism which not only dramatically limited the potential world capitalist market but threatened, in the words of Nikita Khrushchev, 'to bury it.' The phenomenally successful American response was to build a so-called 'free-world market,' based on the dollar and backed up with the atomic bomb.

"Within this market, the free flow of goods was encouraged to provide for the much-needed expansion of American goods and capital. The result was a series of economic miracles that, like the cloud from the big bomb, mushroomed the United States economy to a trillion dollars and lifted devastated Japan, Germany, and Western Europe to new heights of prosperity. Thus the foundation for the rapid growth of the global corporation was laid.

"In the 1960s the ground rules changed radically. It became increasingly evident that the United States lacked the power to eliminate socialist or communist pockets within the global market, even in such weak and obscure places as Vietnam. Certainly the overthrow of the socialist revolutions in either Russia or China by military pressure had become an impossibility. If the integration of either into the new global economy were to be accomplished, it would require other means. To the owners and managers of the new global corporations this meant that attainment of a total, free-world market depended more on their actions and less on governments.

"Now, there is nothing new in merchants exercising political power. The most well-known example was the East India Company, which conquered a sub-continent and ruled over a quarter of a billion people; and of course, the Virginia Company and Plymouth Company helped develop the new world. But the significant difference is that these early trading merchants were *delegated* their political power and were under constant discipline of the Crown. Today's global corporation, by contrast, is operating frequently in opposition to the plans of its base country; and, for all practical purposes, is disciplined only by its insatiable appetite for monetary growth.

"The challenge by the modern corportion has not gone unanswered by the modern nation-state, however. In fact, the governments have assigned prerogatives to themselves unlike anything previously known: the right to manage the economy through control of interest rates, money supply, foreign trade, taxes, quotas, and tariffs; the right to allocate resources within its society; the right to set limits on prices and wages; and the right to subsidize or rescue certain troubled corporations. Waving the banner of national security, the modern state has also demanded the right to control where its citizens may travel and with whom they shall do business—and under what circumstances.

"However, neither the nation-state nor the corporation has attempted to pre-empt the managerial powers exercised by the other; instead, subtly, they have expanded their power together. For the moment, there exists an uneasy truce between these powers. From the global corporation's point of view, the United States government is both a nuisance and a necessity. From the government's point of view, the corporation is a source of national power but, nonetheless, a frustrater of national policy.

"The growth of the global corporation is a story of continuing triumphs of organization and technology over territorial limits. Some sense of how small corporations can afford local loyalities is revealed by the history of corporate expansion in the United States and overseas. The earliest companies, the textile mills, were local in a political sense. They built and managed company towns, and they and the surrounding areas grew together. But these local loyalties were soon transcended as companies outgrew local and regional markets. The ghost towns of the Northeast are reminders of these footloose companies' willingness to sacrifice those communities in their search for ever-expanding markets.

"The relationship of big global corporations and the United States government has steadily degraded over the years. The latest condition is due to the decline of the United States as the preeminent global power. It is now necessary to be more cautious in the choice of friends and in the use of force. It's no longer certain that it is good economic policy to help overthrow governments, as the United States did in countries like Iran or Chile. In the past, whenever and wherever the flag was planted around the world, in some 500 major military and naval bases and in the command posts of over a dozen military interventions, United States corporations have moved in. The construction of a worldwide military empire has, in the past, been good business.

"But the world scene has shifted. The United States, though being severely challenged by Russia, is still the most powerful nation. But it can no longer run the world through either its economic power or its military might. The dollar is no longer king. The power of the State Department, CIA, and Pentagon to make or break governments is not what it was. In fact, there is considerable evidence that both the number one and number two powers are becoming economically weaker through their military policies.

"The goal of corporate diplomacy is replacement of national loyalty with corporate loyalty; it is bidding for this loyalty from workers from many lands who are promised a few pennies more a day than the going wage. To local businessmen in lesser-developed countries it offers participation as local managers, stockholders, and suppliers in a global enterprise with dimensions far beyond anything they could attain in a limited local economy. To governments in similar poor countries, it promises a path to economic growth. But its most powerful appeal is to the general public; and its message is simple and insistent: consumption is the key to happiness and the global corporation offers the products that make life worth living.

"World managers contend that, since the global corporation has become the dominant economic force in the world, the primary function of government is to enable the corporation to fulfill its promise. These duties, they argue, include stabilizing the economy whenever the natural regulating mechanism of the market fails; building and maintaining the necessary roads, harbors, and communication networks; subsidizing, retraining, or moving workers who are displaced by corporations' decisions to seek cheaper labor sources; and finally, acting as co-educators of new labor recruits whenever and wherever needed.

"But the ultimate test of the world manager's global vision is the underdeveloped world. To promote a global vision which bypasses those parts of the planet in which most of the people live, where the problems of survival are starkest, and where political explosions are regular occurrences, is beyond the capacity of even the most accomplished salesman. In their bid for global supremacy, the men who run the global corporations must demonstrate their ability to solve the problems of world poverty.

"But, paradoxically, the underdeveloped world is currently doing more for the advancement of the corporations than the corporations are doing for them. The resources of the poor nations including, incredibly, financial resources; raw materials on and under their territory; cheap labor; and ultimately, potential customers, are increasingly crucial to the plans of the global corporation.

"Why, then, you might ask, are world corporations growing in wealth while the underdeveloped nations continue to languish in poverty? The answer doesn't lie in racial inabilities—in the belief that 'only the dynamic white Westerner is capable of understanding the complexities of modern economics.' The answer does lie in the ability to accumulate what the economists call 'capital stock'; that is, the structures that enable modern, developed societies to function and to create more wealth: roads, communication systems, schools, factories, and machines.

"But capital stock doesn't grow wild. It's the result of specific decisions relating to how to best invest natural resources. Thus, when backward societies begin to produce more than they consume, they cease being static societies and begin the process of growth.

"The essential ingredient in this process is knowledge. It is the introduction of new ways of organizing work—use of a hoe instead of bare hands or a tractor instead of the hoe—that increases human productivity and generates finance capital that can be converted into further increases in productivity in the future.

"But the finance capital generated by the natural wealth of many countries of the underdeveloped world has not been used to build the roads, schools, and factories needed to develop future wealth; but instead, has been siphoned off to the developed world—first as plunder and more recently as dividends, royalties, and fees. The remainder of the finance capital is frequently left in the control of a small local elite who use it to improve their living standard and who invest any surplus abroad. The result has been a process of wealth depletion that has sent many of these primitive economies into a slow, downward spiral.

"One of the most frequently used arguments presented by global corporate managers in substantiating their recent worldwide domination is that they have been responsible for creating hundreds of thousands of new jobs. But unfortunately, exactly the opposite is the truth. Conceding that unemployment figures are the most slippery of statistics, the quantity of people without jobs has actually risen over the last thirty years to the point where something like a third of the available world work force is currently unemployed. Typically, poor countries abound in human resources yet many global corporations continue to export capital-intensive, rather than labor-intensive technology to those countries so that they, the global corporation, can take advantage of local sources of raw materials.

"Recently, when too large a share of the earnings on foreign investment has been permitted to flow out of the countries that controlled the source of scarce raw materials, local political and economic interests have tried to retaliate by forming monopolistic organizations, or cartels, dedicated to reversing the flow of capital. Indeed, from their point of view, organizations such as that currently employed to increase the price of oil in the Near East are really counter-cartels designed only to demand proper payment for materials that are finite and vital to the well-being of the purchaser; and are a form of reparation for years of wanton exploitation. A short while ago, a group was organized in the developed world to counter the counter-cartels. The resultant Trilateral Commission has recruited many of the most highly influential people from the financial and political ranks in the United States, Japan, and Western Europe in an attempt to minimize the friction and competition that divide the giants and make them more vulnerable to the organization of the poor. Thus, the struggle for dominance over the sources of the wealth of the world intensifies."

Once again Thomas Paine halts his pacing and pauses before his two-party class.

"Are there any questions about the material I've just covered?" he asks.

"Yes," answers David. "Are you suggesting that we can't consider the problems of the United States—which is, after all, our self-proclaimed assignment—without also considering the relationship of America's problems to those of the rest of the world?"

"I'm suggesting precisely that, David. Though in the final analysis our corrective plan will be restricted to America and its problems, in the formative stage, we cannot ignore the impact that the rest of the world plays in both the cause and solution of those problems.

"Now, the process by which large corporations use their power to gain increasing control over one sector of the economy and then use that power to gain control over other sectors—a process called cross-subsidization—helps explain how the global corporations have been able to consolidate their positions in such a short period of time.

"There is a particular category of corporation that requires special attention in our quest for solutions to the current bad economic situation. In terms of assets, these corporations are the largest in the world. Can either of you guess what group I'm referring to?"

"Well, Mr. Paine, considering what's been happening in oil these last few years, it's probably the so-called 'seven sisters,' who are now categorized as energy companies," guesses Mary.

"Or perhaps the auto manufacturing companies like General Motors and Ford," adds David.

"For the first time you're both wrong," chortles Tom Paine.

6

Banking and the World Economy

"No one understands the process of economic growth through investment into ever-increasing wider corporate circles better than bankers. In fact, nine of the top ten companies in the United States, in terms of assets—now totalling nearly a half-trillion dollars—are global banks which average well over half of their revenues from foreign transactions.

"Virtually from its inception, a serious debate raged within the United States over the subject of banking. Those who were in a position to know, correctly assessed that those who controlled the purse strings would control the power and wealth of the country," Tom Paine continues.

"We know from our earlier discussions that what appeared to be a happy marriage of political and banking interests took place with the creation of the Federal Reserve System in 1913. To the financially unsophisticated, the Federal Reserve was thought to provide, through its legislated powers, the necessary political discipline over the bankers. But in truth, the Fed was created by bankers for bankers.

"Thus, there is nothing especially mysterious in how banks have grown to awesome size. But what is fascinating, is how they have come to not only dominate the money industry but have also come to dominate many other sectors of the economy as well. The largest banks, such as Citicorp, Bank of America, and Chase Manhattan, now exercize significant influence in many of the country's leading manufacturing and mining companies and, in addition, dominate the transportation industry, the media, and public utilities as well.

"Three strategies have been employed by bankers to achieve this systematic infiltration process. First, is the use of their enormous holdings of industrial stocks which they either own or manage for customers in trust accounts.

"Trust accounts or funds are monies and securities given to banks to manage for estates, pension funds, and charitable institutions. The securities are usually in the form of shares of U.S. corporate stock. For the most part, the banks have been given sole investment responsibility for these securities, which means they can buy and sell the shares at will and vote the stock at shareholders' meetings. Bankers and corporate management are acutely aware that as little as five percent of stock ownership can effectively influence corporate decision-making. Thus, by careful investment practices, the banks have been able to procure stocks that dominate not only many major companies but, in turn, dominate whole sectors of the economy.

"By getting themselves voted onto the board of directors of the companies they control, the bankers gain considerable influence over, for example, where expansion funds will come from. This process is even further enhanced by a second strategy, a process known as interlocking directorates—which simply means that bankers see that other bankers are invited to sit on boards of directors even though those banks may not own stock in that particular company. Through this process, a small but powerful number of financial groups have grown to immense power in the United States.

"The largest and most influential of these financial groups is the Rockefeller-Morgan group, the coordinated financial operations of the descendants, beneficiaries, and employees of John D. Rockefeller and J. P. Morgan. The power base of this empire is six of the country's largest banks, including Chase Manhattan and Morgan Guaranty Trust, which, through their stock control and interlocks, have been able to gain dominance over many of the nation's largest airlines, such as United, American, and Western, and over the three major communication networks of NBC, CBS, and ABC. They also control key sectors of the mining industry; and of course, it hardly seems necessary to mention their involvement in the largest energy corporation in the world, Exxon—which until recently was, of course, Standard Oil.

"The third and most important strategy of banks for extending their influence over the non-banking sectors of the economy has been the use of a process of what the bankers call cross-subsidization. This is simply using the bank's money and influence to enter, and eventually to dominate, unrelated fields such as insurance and equipment leasing. There had been much speculation that dabbling in such unrelated fields by bankers had contributed to the stock market crash in 1929 and accordingly, until the mid-60s banks were effectively precluded from new financial activities.

"The Bank Holding Act of 1956 was designed to reaffirm this principle; but the Act, like others before it, was created by bankers to help bankers. Thus, a rather obvious loophole that permitted non-banking corporations to own both banks and non-related industries was written into the Act. The one-bank holding company which resulted has been used to establish the banking conglomerate in which a single corporation controls literally dozens of related and unrelated business activities. Few acts have ever been implemented that worked more towards further concentrating wealth in the already wealthy. One of the goals of our new comprehensive plan must be to inhibit this kind of legislative folly.

"In the non-government regulated growth industries, the issue isn't whether the banks use their financial power to dictate to the management—basically, they share the same goals of growth and loan repayment. But when we turn to the regulated sectors of the U.S. economy, we find a different picture. These industries, public utilities, airlines, railroads and such, represent essential services to the society and are the foundation on which further economic growth is built. Though technically private firms, they are essentially public trusts that are highly subsidized by the government. They cannot be permitted to go out of business no matter how poorly managed they may be. Needless to say, these companies are favorite targets for bank loans—loans that are in effect guaranteed by the government. In a similar vein, very large corporations like Lockheed and Chrysler have found that, despite their inefficiency and mismanagement, they can ask for and get government loan guarantees similar to public utilities simply because, it is argued, their failure would cause too great a strain on the local economy.

"An analysis of who owns America reveals conclusively that global corporations have gained preeminent power over American society. Managerial control of the technology, finance capital, and tools for developing and disseminating capitalist ideology are now vested in no more than a few hundred hands!

"If global corporations have proven to be incapable of dealing satisfactorily with the major social problems of inflation, unemployment, energy crises, pollution, and so on, why are they permitted to exercise that power? The answer is that there is a structural weakness in the government and other related social institutions.

"But even though the government is proving to be increasingly inefficient due to its sheer size, it is not weak in the same sense Latin American states are weak. Indeed, in many ways the Federal apparatus has grown ever stronger. Yet, big government is unable to corral big business—why?

"Part of the reason lies in the fact that many politicians, due to their background and previous relationships, feel a close affinity for business. Another reason is that the government regulatory agencies have continued to be staffed by personnel from the very industries they are intended to regulate—a classic case of assigning the fox to watch over the chicken coop.

"But, perhaps the strongest reason that government has failed to keep big business in line is that they lack knowledge. The existing disclosure requirements are hopelessly inadequate to permit government to exercise power over global corporations. As a result, the corporations refuse information to government agencies because they claim that it is privileged and confidential. It is utterly impossible to regulate without the knowledge of what it is that is to be regulated.

"Large corporations plan centrally and act globally—nation-states do not. It is this fundamental difference that puts government at a disadvantage in trying to keep up with and control the activities of global corporations. As these corporations become more powerful and mobile, and as their financial statements and operating data reflect less and less economic reality, government finds itself increasingly handicapped in regulating the economy.

"There is an increasingly greater interdependence of the United States economy with other parts of the world economy due to the increase in the globalization process that started in the mid-60s. U.S. global corporations became increasingly dependent upon overseas 'export platforms' for producing goods for the American market and an ever greater percentage of transactions was being integrated into a global intracorporate system that replaced the traditional competitive freemarket system. Overnight transfers of huge cash reserves from one country to another by global corporations and banks increased the difficulty of managing domestic money supplies. For the most part, the total affects of these international transactions on the current financial marketplace is not yet fully understood or appreciated.

"Until the mid-sixties and the onset of so-called 'stagflation,' the use of the monetary tools discussed earlier worked rather well for most of the economy. Despite minor recessions, the United States economy was reasonably stable. Real income climbed for all but those at the bottom of the financial and social ladder; the economy and the stock market grew.

"But then something started to happen. The economy responded less and less to monetary manipulations. When tax credits and other incentives were offered to increase investment, and hence employment and supply of goods, output failed to increase at the anticipated rate; when the Fed raised interest rates or tried to slow increases in the money supply, which was expected to cut demand and reduce inflation pressure, little happened. The reason was that the market had now lost its competitiveness and thus its regulator role as a result of the concentration and globalization of key industries and financial institutions of the United States economy.

"In other words, the strongest global corporations had eliminated most competition either by mergers or outright acquistion and those that were not directly controlled were indirectly pressured from within through their board of directors. No longer, then, is it necessary for these corporations or banks to be sensitive to the increases in interest rates intended to cool the economy; they simply pass the increased cost of raising capital on to the consumer.

"Global corporations and global banks now dominate the international flow of money. The agility and mobility of these resources is enhanced by the global institution's absolute control over the knowledge relating to it. It is now possible, then, for these global giants to operate beyond the effective control of any government and thus frustrate the ability of governments to regulate their economies through either monetary or fiscal policies.

"In December 1971, in response to a worsening trade deficit, the United States devalued the dollar 11 percent. According to financial theory this should have stimulated lagging exports because goods would become more attractive for foreign customers. The balance of trade would be improved by the corresponding rise in the price of imports in the United States.

"But the plan didn't work that way. First of all, devaluation is an economic dirty trick. It simply signals to the rest of the world that American goods and services are not selling as well as theirs; so, the United States will artificially lower the price of its merchandise in relation to theirs. The plan is foolish in that it rarely works—and if it does, it doesn't work for long because the other countries in the market quickly follow suit in the devaluation game. But more important is the fact that the act of cheapening money on the foreign market is no different from cheapening money on the domestic market by printing money—the result, as we know, is inflation.

"The response of the Nixon Administration was to impose price and wage controls. But this action, as it always will, only intensifies the problem. Since prices of goods sold by United

States companies abroad were not subject to controls, more and more scarce items were diverted abroad.

"As we've seen, global corporations and financial institutions have played a major role in frustrating the ability of the United States' financial planners to stabilize the economy. In addition, these global organizations have had a major impact on the American labor movement.

"The actual number of jobs or amount of capital that has been exported overseas is the subject of intense labor and political debate. But the effect that the threat to move has had on labor militancy is not debatable. This loss of bargaining power has unquestionably lessened labor's ability to achieve wage goals in many industries.

"The corporate executive argues that relocation into a cheap labor market overseas is necessary in many cases in order to prevent the takeover of the market by Japanese or European firms. But, even assuming that all foreign investment is defensive, there are ways to protect a market position other than by building a factory in Taiwan.

"For example, companies can put more money into research and development in the United States to replace the diminishing stock of innovative ideas on which future production depends. Such an investment policy would have a greater multiplier effect than foreign investment. Also, United States firms should be cautioned from selling off their comparative advantage to their competitors by licensing technology to them for quick profits. It was this course that allowed the Japanese to hurdle years of research and development time in their successful technological challenge.

"The global corporation in all of its various guises is the most powerful organization ever devised for cutting across international borders. By scanning the entire planet for opportunities and materials, by shifting its management resources from industry to industry and country to country, and by keeping its overriding goal simple—world-wide profit maximization—it has become an institution of unique power.

"The world managers exploit the advantages of capital

mobility, while workers and governments are tied to particular territories. But another name for mobility is rootlessness. By marketing the myth that the pleasures of consumption can be the basis of community, the global corporation helps destroy the true quality of real community—the reaching out of one human to another.

"The underlying reason for the socially disruptive effects of global corporations is that they are still treated as private organizations despite their increasingly public role. Public authorities are incapable of dealing with them because their laws are still based on the old myths of ninteenth-century free-market capitalism. But the free market is largely a historical relic. The concentration of industry and banking, increased involvement of government into private business, and the spectacular rise of global corporations have speeded the decline of the market and further reduced its classic social-regulatory functions.

"The United States-based global corporation has achieved a stage of advanced technology unparalleled in the world. But it should not be forgotten that that technology was assembled with subsidies, tax advantages and other benefits from the public. Further, the social capital of the nation—its air, water and other natural resources—have been expended in the process. Thus, the origin for much of the phenomenal wealth of the global corporation is from public resources and ought to be treated as such!"

7

Constitutional Breakdown and Corporate Government

"I have continued to believe that the history of man's social development should not be thought of as a series of meaningless, aimless, concentric circles; but rather should be characterized as a slow but sure, though sometimes faltering, climb towards an ultimate goal where freedom and equality are responsibly in balance," proclaims Thomas Paine.

"Two centuries ago I felt certain that man was on the threshold of achieving that goal in America. I wrote, 'The birth of a new world is at hand. We have it in our power to begin the world all over again!'

"But when my fellow compatriots met in Philadelphia in that spring of 1787 to draft a new federal constitution, they created a government concerned with special interests instead of national concerns; a government with the John Locke/Montesquieu 'checks and balances' that was intended to constrain those seeking excessive power, but instead created a perennial battle for supremacy between the executive, legislative, and judicial branches of the government. The result has been to divide authority, obstruct creativity, and preclude accountability.

"Until just the last few years, other nonconstitutional forces shielded congressional representatives from existing legislative pressure groups. The most important of these restraining forces was the strong two-party system. For years, the congressional candidate looked to the local and state party machinery for the financing necessary for election campaigns and, when successful, upon arriving at Congress, he found himself firmly under the control of the party chieftains who dominated the numerous committees and party caucuses.

"Pressure groups, or lobbyists, are not new, of course. What is new, is the increase in their numbers that resulted from the surge in government-funded programs which grew out of Lyndon Johnson's 'War on Poverty' and 'Great Society.' Groups formed to work on behalf of the beneficiaries of these new government programs were further augmented by those already lobbying for environmental protection, consumer protection, and so on.

"Special-interest group politics thrives on the proclivity of most congressmen to do whatever gets them the most media exposure, a commodity most believe to be essential to subsequent re-election."

"But, Mr. Paine," interrupts Mary, "isn't such behavior to be expected from representative democracy?"

"Yes, partially," concedes Tom Paine. "But, for representative democracy to be successful it requires the representative to be sensitive to all of his constituents' needs, both at home and nationally. Of special concern here is the fact that the recent failure of most congressmen to act statesmanlike—along with a reaffirmed desire by the citizenry to participate in decision-making that affects his life—has led to a resurgence of participatory democracy.

"The old town house meeting was the original model for this form of democracy—citizens simply meeting together, discussing their needs, and voting in their own best interests. But, significant growth in both the quantity of participants, and area concerned, inevitably led to the process of electing surrogates to do the traveling and voting. Conceptually, it was hoped this system would expand the scope of the elected representative's interests while expanding the geographical area represented.

"The initiative process, now growing in many parts of the nation such as California, is the most recent evidence of the citizenry's lost confidence in its representative's statesmanship. But let us return to this subject shortly," suggests Tom Paine.

"Most of the men who provided input into the structuring of the Constitution professed a belief in the principle that 'all men are created equal.' But what they meant then by the phrase was 'All white, male, property owners are equal under the law.' Little by little, the *principle* has been broadened until the *law* now includes all citizens, irrespective of race, creed, sex, or national origin. But, now it is time to write a constitution that creates a system of government capable of *implementing* this principle and law.

"The current Constitution has proved to be a remarkably resilient document; for a century and a half it stood the test of time. It has not been until the last few years that its deficiences have become increasingly obvious.

"But no one could have predicted that the government that this document authorized would now, two centuries later, *employ* more people than *lived* in all thirteen states in 1787. Or that the government would represent a population that would someday approach a quarter of a *billion* people. Or that government property would someday extend around the globe. Or that great global corporations would evolve to challenge the government itself for supremacy. Or that America would face global military powers that employ weapons capable of near-instant, total annihilation. Or that there would come the time that the government would be expected to produce one hundred million jobs for men *and women*. Or that advances in technology would produce global networks of oral and video communication systems. Or transportation systems capable of circumnavigating the earth in hours, rather than in months or years.

"The list of mind-boggling changes since the creation of the Constitution is virtually endless. But, as we've seen in our discussions, not only has the government created by the Constitution been challenged by problems relating to external growth, it has been assaulted internally by subtle, but critical, changes in social and economic behavior."

"Mr. Paine," interjects Mary, "I've listened intently to your dissertation; admittedly struggling at times to comprehend all of the multifaceted national problems you've explored. Throughout, I've mentally sought the identity of the public enemies responsible and, as you've noticed, continued to gravitate towards the same one—government. So I'm not surprised to hear you suggest the need for a new constitution. In fact, considering your past involvement in American, French, and English government formation I suspect that you already have a new government outlined in your mind."

"Yes, I must confess that your suspicion is justified, Mary. In fact, I have what I believe to be the ultimate organization in mind."

"Mr. Paine, I'm extremely anxious to hear more about your plan," David excitedly adds. "But before you start into it, I'd like to comment on your earlier discussion relating to representative versus participatory democracy. I, for one, am intrigued by the possibilities now available for direct involvement of the citizenry in the operation of its government. I believe strongly that, technologically, the time is ripe, and equally as important, that the citizens themselves are now mentally prepared to play such a direct role."

"I wholeheartedly agree, David. I know you must have in mind the recent innovation in television that permits viewer response to specific questions and polls. Undoubtedly, this advance will be available nationwide in a relatively short time, thus making improved forms of it available for individual participation in the fascinating 'game' of politics.

"Now, Mary and David, we've covered a number of topics related to the nation's current breakdown in social and political institutions. There are still numerous others; education, medical, law enforcement, to name a few, that must ultimately be considered. But, I'd like to delay their consideration until I'm well into my new government plan.

"As you will see, the government structure I'm about to outline is so thoroughly adaptable it will greatly diminish the stresses causing many of these peripheral problems in any event. But again, I cannot stress too strongly the need to subject every detail of my plan to the probing criteria of whether it meets the needs of all the citizenry, individually and collectively. We must not lose sight of the fact that governments are created by men for men. In most previous historical cases, the government, once created, soon became the master rather than the slave. It is our objective here to reverse this historical trend.

"Earlier, you'll recall," continues Tom Paine, "we took a somewhat critical look at corporations, particularly those operating globally. We noted how, in relatively few years, they had virtually outgrown the disciplines, constraints, and allegiance of, and to, their base governments.

"Now, there are many logical reasons for this growth; not the least of which is their singular focus on profit as a motivational force; coupled with technological breakthroughs that enhanced their worldwide mobility and communication capability. But the prime element motivating their growth was the evolution of the modern corporate structure, an organizational structure that clearly identifies each employee's role in the management pyramid: his identity, authority, and responsibilities. Therefore, each person in this superior organizational structure is certain of who he is responsibile for and who he is responsible to. With this operational superiority in mind, and with the desire to recognize and put in use the most advanced thinking, I have molded my plan to fit a modified corporate structure.

"The modification must consider several recent national trends. For example, it must recognize that America is now an information society—no longer an industrial society. Thus, government must provide for rapid movement both vertically and horizontally within the corporate structure. Also, the new structure must be sensitive to the growing democratization of the workplace. Workers—in and out of government—are correctly demanding greater voice in decision-making."

"Well," agrees David, "I can certainly see merit in your suggestion to model the new government along the lines of a corporation; but I, for one, would oppose designing it as a profit-seeking organization. As you know even better than I, in a capitalistic society, profit is the result of risk, and risk results from competition; and I don't believe we ought to further encourage direct head-to-head competition between governments. I hope whatever design we agree on will ease international tensions—not further intensify them!"

"Your point is well taken, David; and, as I see Mary's head nodding affirmatively, I can assume we are all in agreement on the point.

"Now, let me briefly outline what I have in mind. One of the many planning and statistical groups operating out of Washington, D.C., collects and arranges its national data so that it is able to recognize various statistical, social, and financial changes occurring in concise geographical areas not unlike the ancient Greek city-states. Each of these areas has a metropolitan center that serves as the focal point for all business and cultural activity. These analysts regularily track and project, for example, shifts in population, employment, and income in each of some one hundred and eighty-four economic areas in America. My plan would utilize this, or a similar arrangement of what I have renamed Central Service Areas, as the base of my tri-level government pyramid. Each Central Service Area will serve as the coordinating center for employment, education, shopping, utility services, grass-root politics and recreational and cultural activities.

"The second level of the new government will consist of six Regionals each containing a reasonably balanced quantity of Central Service Areas. In this balancing process, I considered people-oriented criteria such as population, employment, and income trends; for the most part ignoring geographical size. The Regionals are organized so that they run in vertical slices of the country; north to south, or top to bottom. This arrangement is designed to minimize the effect of recent and future migrations of people and businesses from colder to warmer climates. A centrally located Regional capital is to act as a computer center for the control and collection of my new and original Variable Instantly-applied Transaction (VIT) tax. However, to fully utilize the computer capability, it will also coordinate national elections and annual and tri-annual policy reviews that will be discussed shortly.

"The third, and highest, level of government will be centered in the current capital, Washington, D.C. This level will incorporate the use of a chief executive, national board of directors, and ten federal departments.

"I'm sure that even this brief glimpse has whetted your curiosity, Mary and David. You should have many questions regarding my unique tri-level corporate-structured government; and of course, I will attempt to resolve each question."

"But for now, I believe it will be more meaningful if I give time to examine these several charts that graphically depict the details of the government I've just introduced."

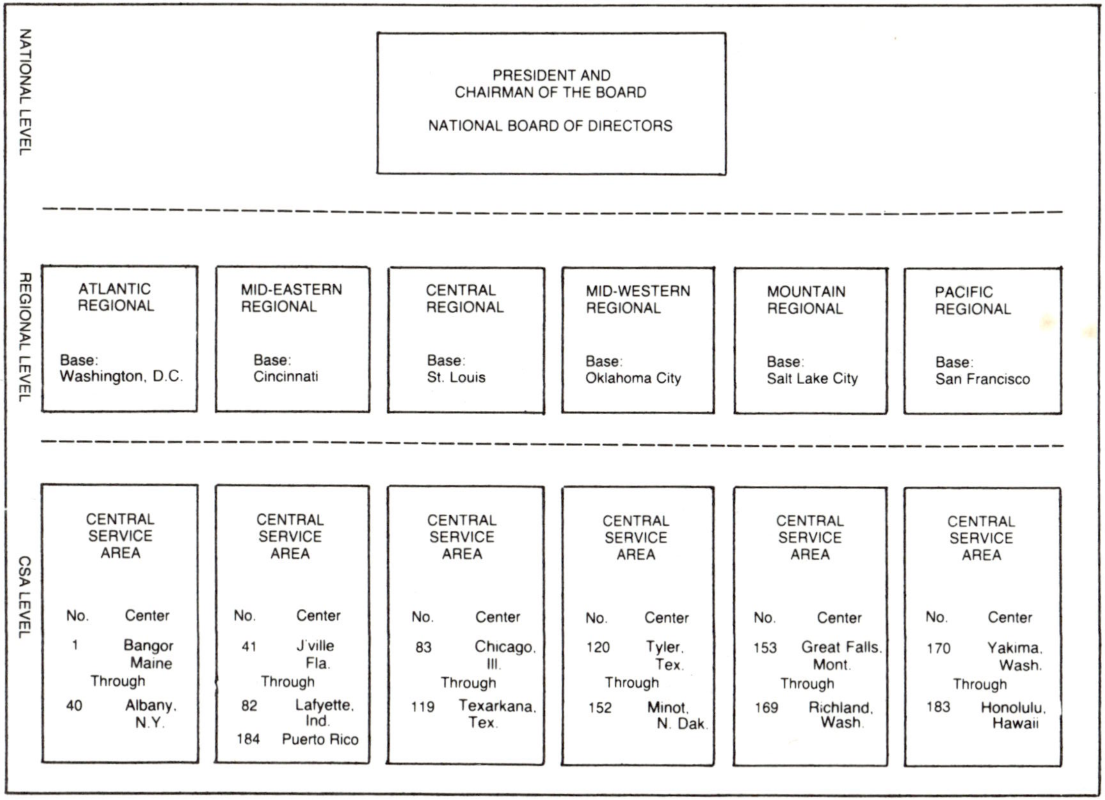

Figure 1. Example of Tri-level Corporate Government

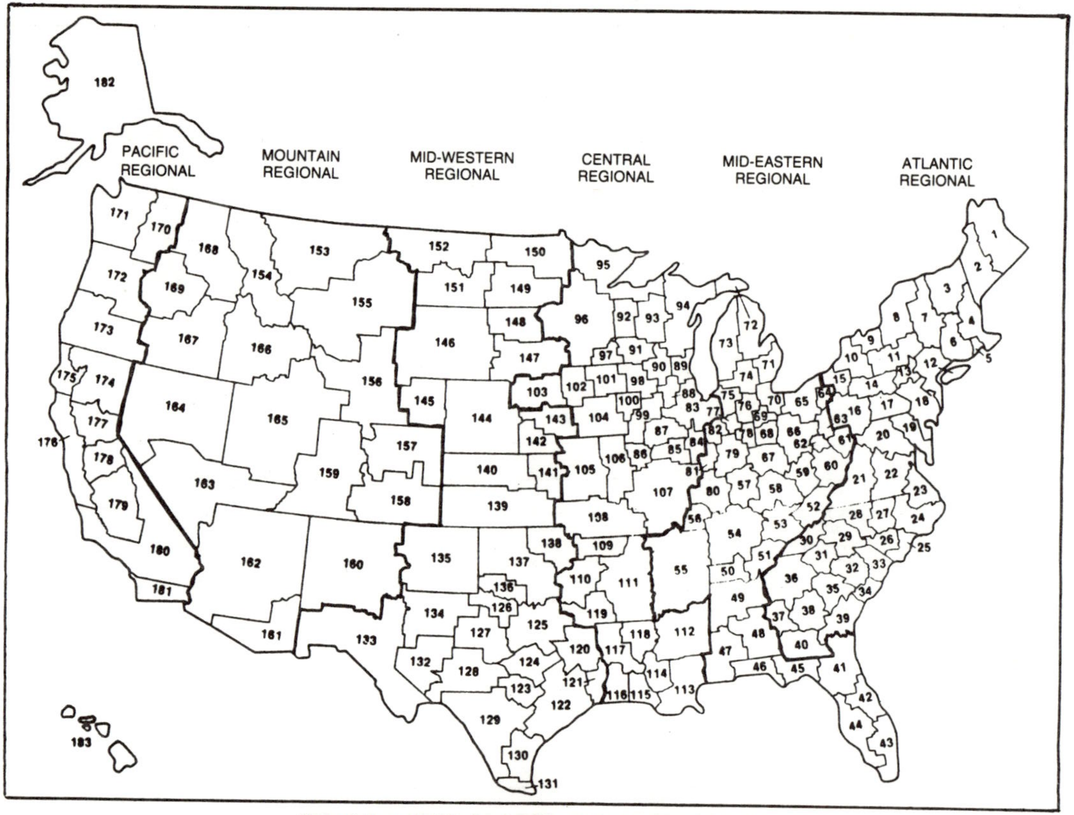

Figure 2. Example of Regional and Central Service Area Distribution

Source: National Planning Association, *Basic Maps of the U.S. Economy, 1967–90.*

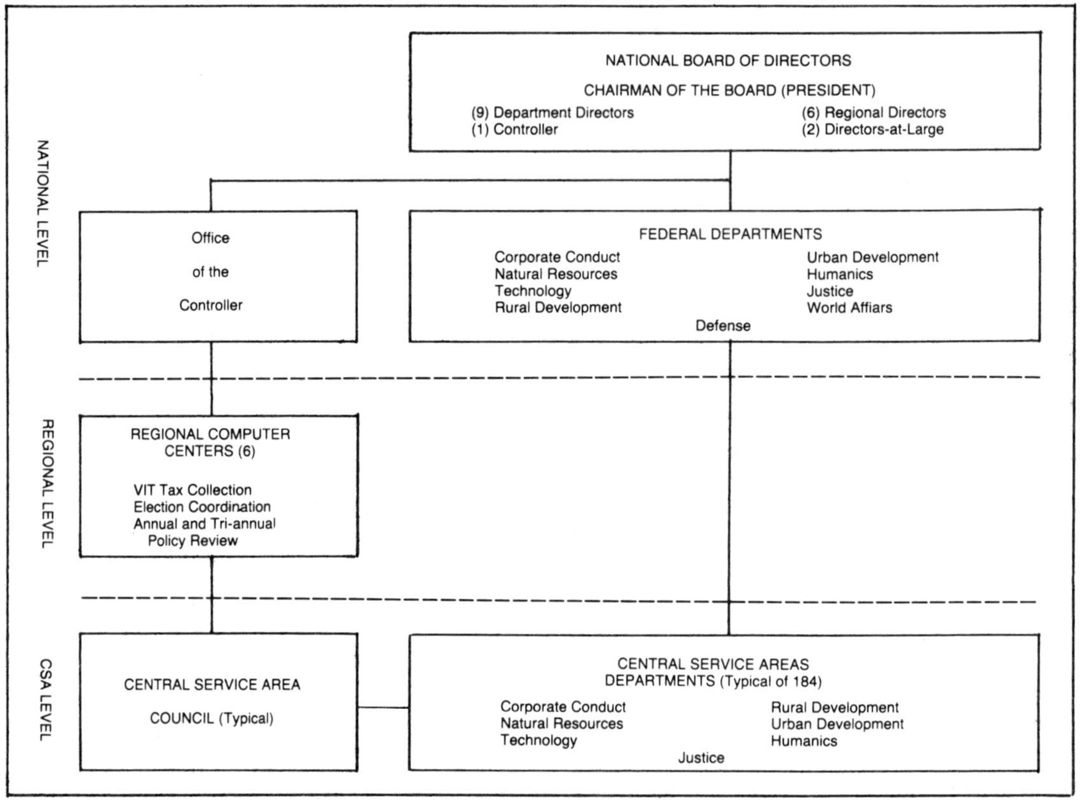

Figure 3. Task Implementation

8

A New Economic Structure

"Do I denote a hint of acceptance in your expressions, or is that simply a look of bewilderment?" smilingly queries Tom Paine.

"Well, initially, I like what I've seen and heard," ventures a thoughtful David. "But I still have numerous questions relating to who does what. At this moment, though, my curiosity is focused on the make-up of the ten federal agencies shown on your charts, Mr. Paine."

"Fair enough," nods the new government planner. "I had first planned to describe the responsibilities and authority of each official, starting with those of the President; but let's accede to your curiosity, David, by describing the make-up of the federal departments first. It is certainly true that they represent one of the keys to the success of my plan.

"It's important to understand at the outset that these departments are intended to be both planning and operational agencies. In other words, they are intended to accomplish tasks, not just formulate ideas. However, the departments are to derive their authority from policies established by the National Board of Directors.

"What exists now is the not unexpected result of the attempt by my compatriots to compromise previous deficiencies by balancing the power among three governmental branches—the Executive, Legislative, and Judicial.

"The resultant jockeying for supremacy of these three branches has been one of the principal causes of the ever expanding bureaucracy—the most recent example being the burgeoning legislative staffs.

"While the politicians are distracted with their defensive internal conflicts, the interests of their constituency are frequently overlooked.

"There are other equally critical deficiencies that have developed as the result of this trilateral form of government—failure to share data, personnel, and funds, for example—but the most important consequence of this rivalry is the present fear of failure and reluctance to act!

"It is the recognition of these failures, then, that has created the need for a more responsive form of government—one patterned after the thoroughly tested corporate structure.

"So, with this prologue, let's first look at the department concerned with financial matters, the Office of the Controller. As we discovered earlier, much of the nation's problems, whether political, social, or economic, are the direct or indirect result of improper monetary controls.

"Also noted earlier, for two-thirds of a century the Federal Reserve System has failed its legislative assignments to cushion economic downturns, eliminate inflation and unemployment, and stabilize the nation's monetary system—and continued authority to try simply cannot be justified. Therefore, the Federal Reserve System must be eliminated!

"As a replacement, my plan calls for the establishment of a corporation-like controller's office designed to monitor the volume of money and credit in the nation, and report the resultant data and recommendations to the National Board of Directors. But, unlike the Fed, it will not be permitted to take unilateral action; but instead, it will act on specific orders of the Board only.

"Referring again to our earlier verbal explorations, we see that if money is to perform its proper function in the marketplace, it must be both stable and acceptable. *Stability* requires that it not fluctuate significantly in relative terms—and, as we should now know, discipline requires diligent control over the *quantity*, or volume, of money and credit. *Acceptability* is related principally to its *quality*, and of course, quality is a function of money's backing or collateral.

"As a brief aside, let me comment on the recent dire media suggestions relating to the possibility that America may soon go bankrupt. No one really knows what the word 'bankruptcy' means when applied to a nation, but it is an economic fact, that no one, whether person, company, or country, can involuntarily go into bankruptcy when his (its) assets vastly exceed his (its) liabilities; and such is the case in contemporary America; for, despite all its problems, the nation is the wealthiest country in the world. Its physical assets are estimated to be a staggering ten *trillion* dollars! In the current year, this amounts to approximately forty-three thousand dollars for every American.

"Now, let's return to the subject of money quality. Because it is necessary to re-establish a firm base for the nation's monetary system, and because the quantity of gold is no longer adequate to this task alone, the new government will pledge all of its assets, including the value of its land resources—and, of course, its gold and silver—as monetary backing for financial transactions that utilize dollars for payment.

"To even further strengthen the nation's monetary system, as well as to restrain the government from future monetary manipulations, such as devaluation, it will become the law of the land to permit payment of all legal debts, using any of the stable currencies of the world—the pound, franc, mark, or yen, for example—in addition to the dollar, of course. As you can imagine, this will ultimately help stabilize each of these monetary units, including the dollar, because if any of the governments originating these currencies fails to keep its monetary system in rein, the unit will quickly fall into disfavor as a means of exchange in the international marketplace."

"Down with inflation and hail the new stable dollar!" cheer David and Mary in unison.

"Now come some elements of my plan that I expect to be

even more controversial," warns Tom Paine. "As we discussed earlier, approximately half of the soon-to-be trillion dollar annual national budget is involved with what has come to be called transfer payments—money intended to partially redistribute the country's wealth. But, in spite of the unprecedented increases in these payments over recent years, this egalitarian goal is further from being achieved than ever.

"Equally as important are the millions of recipients who quietly think of themselves as 'being on the dole,' who are, as a result, discouraged from seeking gainful employment, adequate housing, or meaningful education. In spite of this spiritual decay, though, one fact is inescapable—the country cannot permit the gap between the haves and have-nots to grow wider. Presently, half of the wealth of the country is owned by less than one fifth of the people, while the bottom fifth are living well below a generally recognized subsistence level.

"To attack this problem of inadequate wealth distribution head-on, my plan calls for the formation of a Personal Capital Account for every citizen, irrespective of age.

"It will work like this: preceding the inauguration of the plan, all citizens will complete a simple questionnaire establishing each person's net worth. The form will call for all assets—things totally or partially owned—to be listed in one column, and all liabilities—debts owed—to be listed in a second column. The difference between the totals of the two columns being the individual's net worth. To the net worth value established in each nineteen-year-old-or-older citizen's Personal Capital Account, will be debited an arbitrary, one-time 30 thousand dollars. Each person age eighteen and under will receive a pro-rata share for each year of age. Please note: this credit or addition is to be made to each citizen's account irrespective of the size of his net worth.

"Further, life insurance companies will be required to refund all premiums previously received on death policies. These companies will then cease issuing additional insurance policies payable on death. This refund will become part of the net worth of each recipient. In principle, after-death insurance is an unfair tax on the living; but, fair or not, as you will see, it simply will no longer be necessary.

"For just a few moments, let me stray from the direct line of the current discussion and explore who owns the land in America. A recent government survey determined that about 40 percent of the U.S. land area of 2.3 billion acres is owned by government—federal, state, and local, leaving sixty percent in private hands. Half of the privately owned land is held by 1 percent of the landowners. About thirty percent of the privately held land has been acquired since 1970. Most owners are white, between the ages of fifty and sixty-four and are males—but the last fact ignores husband-wife joint ownership.

"Now, if we look more closely at the private half owned by only one percent of the owners, we find that the ownership, whether by individuals, partnerships, or corporations, is even more skewed when viewed from the opposite direction; about seventy-five percent of the owners—mostly small residential lot-owners—hold only three percent of the land.

"While it is true that land ownership is not the critical problem in America that it is in much of the rest of the world—a literal handful of entities own most of the land in Latin America and South American countries, for example—the trend toward fewer and larger landowners needs to be reversed.

"To accomplish this reversal, the computation of individual net worth will exclude any consideration for land or estimated value for what lies below the surface of the land. Both will subsequently become the combined property of all the citizenry and be held in trust by the national corporation-state. All man-made improvements above ground, however, will continue to be owned by whoever holds title to them. The land needed by persons or corporations presently utilizing it will be leased back to them at nominal rates. This plan will have the affect of retrieving, for the citizens, the vast land-holdings that were virtually given away over the years to various individuals and corporations such as railroad interests, oil companies, and land developers that were able to take advantage of the then transient need and legislative pressures. Parcels of land lying under the citizen's primary residence or farm will be leased back at no cost, however.

"And now for what may well be the most controversial part of my plan—no individual's net worth will be permitted to exceed one million dollars! Any excess beyond this amount will automatically be deleted and credited to the new government's general account. This provision is designed to make available to society unused and unneeded funds while continuing to encourage individual competitiveness. This upper individual limit on wealth will permit accumulation of estates up to reasonable limits; it is not designed to eliminate mansions and yachts—only to assure wider sharing of them."

"Wow, Mr. Paine, I don't know about David, but I feel the way I might if I were being served a ten-course meal. Each disclosure is a new exciting surprise and each arrives before I've stopped savoring the preceding course," gasps Mary. "I personally like your plan, which re-establishes a firm base for the nation's monetary system and makes America's currency competitive with other international currencies. But I'm still having trouble chewing the part about redistribution of wealth. How will the recipient use the money once he has it in his account?"

"Well," continues Tom Paine patiently, "before I directly answer your question, Mary, let me briefly comment on the subject of *complex* taxation. As we know, increasing the size of the tax-bite can have definite negative consequences: a lowering of work incentives and an encouragement of alternative market modes—a return to the barter system, for example. But rarely does anyone comment on the severe strain today's excessively complex tax system places on the positive utilization of available personal time. I have observed, with increasing frustration, how individual and business taxpayers have been forced to expend ever increasing time and effort on decisions relating to tax consequences, rather than expending management time on the reliability or quality of the product or service to be provided.

"In addition, the complexity of the tax system has mandated an increase in the quantity of accountants and attorneys required to provide adequate tax counsel.

"Thus, the increasingly complex tax system itself is a growing cause for the decrease in America's productivity, and becoming a major new segment of the total tax burden.

"Now, back to Mary's query. The plan affirms that with two minor exceptions, there will be only one tax and that it will be so simple as to require little or no surveillance by either the taxpayer or outside counsel. This tax, to be named, you'll recall, a Variable Instantly-applied Transaction tax, relies upon the recent marvels of the computer industry for its existence and subsequent success.

"It will work this way: Each citizen will be issued a Lifetime Identification and Finance (LIF) card that will be his own individual key to his Personal Capital Account. Virtually all transactions will be conducted utilizing this card to debit or credit the individual's account.

"The VIT tax, which will be applied to all purchases, whether goods or services, will replace all existing taxes—sales, property, excise, or corporate—and will initially be applied at twenty-five percent of the value of any transaction and gradually lowered to twenty percent or under, over five or six years. To put these numbers in perspective, it is estimated that the twenty-five percent rate applied today would net the government approximately four hundred billion dollars. It is further estimated that the overall tax burden is costing each taxpayer about half of his current earnings.

"It's important to note that tremendous decreases in government costs and expenditures are certain, as the new, more efficient government becomes totally functional.

"As mentioned earlier, politicians continue to vote expenditures that increasingly cause deficit spending—the national debt having now passed the trillion dollar mark—but attempt to shroud the effect of these actions by decreasing the monetary value of the growing national debt through a process called 'monetizing'—a fancy name for monetary devaluation resulting from inflation. To preclude such action in the future, my plan permanently eliminates national debt; it merely declares the nationally-owed portion of the debt null and void, and requires that all subsequent budgets are not to be exceeded.

"So, as you can start to see, with welfare payments gone, payments on the national debt eliminated, operational costs of government sharply lowered, and defense appropriations cut in half through sharp reductions in international stress—more about this later—in addition to the other monetary stabilizing actions explained earlier, the true value of the dollar will more than double while taxation is being halved!"

"It's starting to sound very good, Mr. Paine. However, as a woman, I'm especially interested in your vision of tomorrow's day-to-day shopping," grins Mary.

"All right, then, in keeping with our declared intent, the plan consistently considers the wants and needs of everyday living. In addition, the plan desires to not unduly inhibit the free marketplace. Thus, currency and coin for small transactions will be available through the convenient monetary vending machines located throughout the Central Service Areas. By simply inserting the individual's LIF card, and replying to preprogrammed queries, money in incremental amounts of one hundred dollars will be provided—if available in the individual's personal account, of course.

"Since there will be no taxes charged on small transactions, the Regional computer will apply the current VIT tax to the requested amount and adjust the Personal Capital Account accordingly. Incidentally, the computer will provide a confidential summary of the individual's current account upon request."

"Okay," cautiously observes David, "I concede that your plan has considerable merit. It certainly addresses many of the problems we encountered in our earlier discussions and provides plausible, even if sometimes controversial, solutions to most. But one component of your plan continues to worry me: how can a thirty-thousand-dollar payment be made to each citizen without causing significant inflation in itself?"

"The same question caused me a great deal of concern, David," responds a somber Tom Paine. "The redistribution segment is quite frankly the keystone of my plan. But until I was confident that it could be accomplished without inflationary consequences, I was unwilling to suggest any part of the plan.

"However, I'm now confident that the resolution of both of our concerns lies in an understanding of the timing of the action and of the purpose for which it is being accomplished.

"We'll recall that the definition of inflation related the quantity of money and credit to the amount of goods and services available; and we'll recall, too, that in recent years the two sides of the monetary/supply equation were operating in direct opposition to the desired goal—money and credit being regularily and systematically increased while production of goods and services was decreasing.

"Unquestionably, with the implementation of this overall plan, a complete reversal in both sides of the equation will occur: the quantity of money and credit will stabilize while goods and services are increasing as a result of the anticipated dynamic upsurge in productivity.

"Also, let me add that this debit, the thirty thousand dollars, is basically a one-time, long-term adjustment in personal wealth, and as such, is in lieu of all previous short-term government compensations made in the form of welfare payments, social security benefits, tax incentives, pension compensation, and so on. As the citizenry comes to realize the singular nature of the adjustment through pre-event announcements, they will see the necessity of carefully budgeting the money over a relatively long time span.

"In addition, all of the other anti-inflation actions—balanced budgets, lowered taxes, stabilized monetary system—will be implemented simultaneously. For these reasons, I am confident, David, that the redistribution segment of my plan can be accomplished without causing renewed eruptions of catastrophic inflation."

9

Corporate Disciplines, Natural Resources, and Technological Incentives

"The second new federal department to be described is the Department of Corporate Conduct," resumes Tom Paine.

"If you recall our earlier discussions relating to global corporations and the increasing lack of international restraints on their activities, you must share my eagerness to see that this agency is provided with just the proper balance of corporate responsibilities and disciplines.

"We noted earlier how the superior pyramid design of the modern corporation had enhanced its ability for rapid growth.

"But in addition, this structure aids today's companies in coping with swiftly changing, increasingly complex events occurring around the globe. Without this ability, global corporations would find it impossible to successfully compete with highly dynamic companies from countries like Japan, whose industrial strength lies in its blend of cooperation among business, government, and labor.

"Thus, in keeping with our new corpra-state, and to provide the best possible atmosphere for sound market activity, I recommend that businesses consisting of two or more persons, whether private or public, national or international, be converted to corporate form.

"As an aside, the recent trend for business activity to be conducted via limited partnerships is in direct opposition to our goal of improving the balance of wealth existing in the nation. Only those already relatively wealthy are generally in position to gain by being limited partners and investors.

"Some rather curious changes in work behavior have been occurring in recent years. As the physical demands have lessened and the amount of time spent on the job decreased, employees have become more disillusioned with their role in the marketplace.

"The reasons for this behavior are complex—high taxation, acting as a disincentive; increased automation, adding to the boredom of the tasks; and the vagaries of the economy, raising anxiety levels, to name but a few.

"But irrespective of what explanations are offered, there is only one act that can be expected to positively remotivate all sectors of the marketplace—direct coupling of the employee's destiny with that of his company by requiring that all profit-making corporations be owned by their employees!

"Thus, with most business being conducted by corporations, the economy can take advantage of this more responsive mode; and, with those corporations converted to employee-owned companies, presently-lacking productivity can be greatly enhanced.

"The conversion process should go like this: Each employee will be issued one share of common stock for each five years of service. Where a pension fund, retirement fund, or savings plan exists, it will be used to wholly or partially compensate the company for the sale of stock to the employees. In the absence of such funds, a long-term stock purchase and repayment plan will be initiated on behalf of the employees.

"Members of the Board of Directors of the employee-owned company will be elected by, and from, the employees. The Board of Directors will secure the most competent management available and provide direction and overall operational goals and objectives for the company's future. Beyond any doubt, questions relating to relocation of facilities or product lines will be weighed very carefully by the employee-controlled Board of Directors. The direct employee representation on the company's

Board of Directors will eliminate the need for labor unions, of course.

"The Department of Corporate Conduct will encourage corporations to decrease the standard workweek to 32 hours and provide longer and more frequent vacations. Shorter work periods will help decrease the problem of industrial boredom and also help assure full employment throughout the nation. However, the problem of unemployment will be radically reduced, in any case, as employees come to realize that their savings are now secure and stable and that they can, therefore, safely plan for retirement at an early age.

"Though it is expected that partial ownership in a company will greatly increase the employee's interest, motivation, and loyalty he will not be precluded from moving to other jobs, if he so chooses. When, and if, an employee elects to leave, he will receive an estimated pro-rata share of the company's current net worth.

"Each corporation chartered as a profit-making company by the Department of Corporate Conduct will be required to show a regular profit. Failure to do so for five consecutive years will result in denial of charter renewal. It simply should not be the intent of the newly revitalized government to bail out or attempt to prolong the existence of mismanaged or financially sick companies.

"The Department of Corporate Conduct will also require complete disclosure of data relating to corporate operations. The submitted data will include financial information relating to dealings at all corporate levels and at all locations, national or international. The corporation will also be required to provide comprehensive and accurate data relating to the source of all materials owned, leased, or contracted for. This provision is specifically designed to preclude further withholding of data vital to the nation's future well-being. It has become obvious that the current lack of reliable data prevents meaningful, long-term national planning.

"In a similar vein, submittal of drawings and data relating to the amount and price of labor used to produce overseas, products destined for the American market, will be required. When this information indicates that a substantial variance exists in the manufacturing cost due primarily to lower wages at the overseas production site, the price of the import will be adjusted accordingly. No other impediment to free trade will be permitted, however; certainly it is in the best interest of all Americans that they have the opportunity to buy the best products available in the global marketplace. But it's not in their best interest to encourage relocation of manufacturing facilities to other areas simply because these so-called 'export platforms' presently utilize cheap labor pools or possess a temporary abundance of local raw materials. It goes almost without saying that *jobless* Americans are financially incapable of buying merchandise irrespective of where it's from or how good or cheap it may be.

"To aid in determining the success of this program, all overseas divisions of global corporations will be required to disclose profits from those operations separate from the parent company. Fifty percent of the profits resulting from the overseas operations will be returned to the host country it came from. The current policy of most global corporations of consuming the host country's raw materials and labor without ample compensation must cease.

"In addition, any future relocation of plants or facilities will require the moving concern to compensate the Central Service Area vacated for any resultant social costs.

"If I hear no questions, the third national agency to be discussed will be the Department of Natural Resources." Tom Paine pauses, looks expectantly, then resumes.

"Until recently the nation was blessed with an adequate supply of most raw materials necessary for its use; but increasingly, America has become more dependent upon other areas of the world for its supply of strategic materials.

"So, with an adequate supply of reliable information from the national data bank, this department can conduct the necessary analyses for reliable long-term planning for supply of critical raw materials and land resources. When, and if, shortages are forecast, programs designed to provide alternates will promptly be recommended to the National Board for consideration.

"Also, when conditions warrant, this agency, with the proper authorization, will take short-term action as a counter-cartel. The extreme danger to the nation resulting from the recent OPEC-induced oil shortages could have been considerably lessened, for example, if the national government had acted as sole purchaser of all of its domestic oil requirements similar to the method presently being used to acquire the special reserve oil being stockpiled in the southern salt caverns.

"The smooth transition from one era to another in such critical fields as energy can only be assured through consistent, reliable, and timely national planning.

"One of the most critical natural resources being wantonly misused is land. This is especially true of agricultural land and vividly points up the need for a national land survey and allocation program. Due to obvious irreplaceability, the nation—and, indeed the world—can no longer afford the luxury of covering arable land with buildings, parking lots, or streets. This serious problem has been amplified in recent years, as additional millions of acres have been arbitrarily excluded from future use by declaring them permanent parks or scenic areas.

"There is sufficient land available in America to satisfy all of its various needs—including residential, agricultural, recreational, and industrial—but, only if it is sanely allocated to its most appropriate use. It must be recognized that certain land should become recreational or scenic only after it has given up other precious resources—particularily coal, oil, or mineral.

"Another critical commodity that must be carefully surveyed and allocated, is water. Frequently the fact is overlooked that no real shortage of this product exists. What does exist is a severe problem relating to the distribution of it. It is a fact that there is exactly the same amount of this liquid necessity available now as existed when people first set foot on the planet.

"However, it should be noted that man is failing to properly use even the potable water delivered to it by nature. Only about half of the water landing on the western side of the continental divide is ever used constructively by man, for example; the other half is simply returning untouched to the ocean from which it originated. This fact should obviate the need for inconspicuous redistribution plants to be built at the mouths of rivers and streams.

"With national attention focused on the most appropriate use of all the nation's natural resources—mineral, land, water, and air—plans can be developed to provide sufficient quantities of each for years to come.

"Almost everyone is familiar with the remarkable story of the discovery of penicillin, how in 1928, Alexander Fleming's 'magic bullet' came to him through the open window of his English laboratory in the shape of a mold which landed on a microbial colony of staphylococcus and dissolved them.

"From this deceptively simple incident can be plucked two important observations. First, Fleming's penicillin mold is readily comparable to ideas that are eternally adrift everywhere, and second, those ever-present ideas can never be realized unless, like Fleming's laboratory, a proper environment is made available to receive and nurture them.

"Indeed, it is ideas—moments of reflection, some say—that differentiate man from all other creatures of the world. And, in fact, as we know, the earth itself is mankind's exclusive ideas laboratory.

"America as a nation was created out of ideas; and, because it will soon be receptive again to advanced inspirational concepts, it will shake off its current foolish fears of inadequacy and resume its rightful leadership role throughout the world.

"The Department of Technology will be the nation's collector of innovative ideas. But it won't stop there, for the Department will coordinate and fund all viable research and development among its sister departments and all other public or private interests.

"There literally is no limit to the technological advances possible in America. The energy problem, for example, will ultimately be solved when nuclear fusion is perfected soon after the turn of the century. In the interim, the country's energy needs must be met by utilizing currently available sources of energy from petroleum, gas, coal, thermal, solar, and nuclear.

"But less spectacular changes will become regular occurrences in every field: travel will become much safer as collision-avoidance systems are designed and perfected for autos, trucks, trains, aircraft, and ships; health will improve and life expectancy will increase dramatically, as cures for most of man's illnesses—including cancer and coronary diseases—are found; the workplace and home will be revolutionized as new automated tools and appliances spring into being.

"The list of new creative inventions and discoveries is limited only by man's ingenuity and the Department of Technology will provide every possible encouragement—technical as well as financial—to all capable individuals or companies.

"I've noted your eagerness to ask additional questions, Mary and David," pauses Tom Paine, "but I would like to briefly postpone additional questions until all of the federal departments have been described. I believe some of your queries will be resolved along the way—even as new ones come to mind."

10

Government and the Human—His Environment, Personal Needs, Legal Status, and World Interface

"The offices of both Urban and Rural Development will attack problems relating to living in either country or city environments. You will both agree, I'm sure, that only those who have lived in both can fully appreciate the variety of challenges existing in each.

"First of all, though, the current situation that sees increasing quantities of young adults precluded from purchasing their own homes or farms must end. The backbone of the nation's societal structure is the family unit and home ownership, even if on leased land, and it is one of the most cohesive elements necessary to hold this vital body together. To correct this condition, these two departments will make available low-interest, long-term loans for purchase of homes whether located in a condominium, on a city lot, or the component of farm acreage.

"Irrespective of which environment is chosen, problems do arise, of course. Thus, those living in rural areas continue to need the most current information available relative to methods for improving water systems, waste disposal systems, or drainage systems; while city-dwellers regularly need advice on coping with traffic, crime, or unsanitary air. These, and similar problems, can best be resolved by departments designed specifically to meet them head-on.

"Throughout the nation, the cores of most cities are decaying. As these areas have degenerated with age, those who could have fled to the suburbs; taking with them the financial means for supporting even minimal maintenance of buildings, streets, or services.

"Many social, financial, and political rejuvenation programs have been tried, but, for the most part, have failed. However, in spite of these degenerating conditions, a significant segment of the citizenry continues to live in the cities—some because they can't afford other alternatives, others, because they sincerely enjoy and desire the interrelationships that this mode of living offers.

"Unfortunately, with today's financial climate being what it is, there is little internal motivation to change or improve living conditions within America's cities. But I am confident that a sharp reversal of these negative conditions will occur as this plan takes affect and incomes and jobs increase, taxes decrease, and money values stabilize.

"The Department of Humanics is intended to relate to those conditions especially concerned with maintaining and improving the human environment—man's medical, educational, cultural, and recreational needs.

"There's no immediate relief in sight from the skyrocketing costs of medical care. Current estimates would have one anticipate that health-care expenses will soar to over three thousand dollars per person per year by 1990. Of this amount, doctor's bills are expected to be over six hundred dollars and hospital cost over fourteen hundred dollars. Total cost to the nation—over eight hundred billion dollars per year!

"These numbers demand that the time has come for the government to provide, at public expense, *essential* medical and dental services for its citizenry. These services will be provided through Health Maintenance Organizations located in each Central Service Area. HMOs are clinic-like organizations staffed and equipped to treat most common ailments. By containing many doctors, nurses, and staffs within a single facility properly equipped with, and utilizing, common diagnostic equipment, great savings in the cost of medical services are possible.

"When it is determined through examination at an HMO that more extensive treatment is necessary, the patient will be referred to specialized in-patient facilities. The costs of this advanced treatment will be borne by the patient and his group insurance carrier as provided through his employer, school, or retirement organization.

"Dental services should be provided utilizing the same approach to cost—basic services being made available at the Health Maintenance Organization but with cosmetic straightening and capping being performed outside, at individual expense.

"Considering the recent sharp increase in medical costs throughout the country, it is essential that the potential patient be reintroduced into the cost-consideration cycle. By making the potential patient responsible for advanced treatment, an essential brake to these burgeoning costs will again be applied.

"As was noted earlier, the American educational system is in deep trouble. Correctly seen as a key to the better life, minority groups, such as the blacks, have pressed strongly for schools that could provide learning services equal to those provided for white children. When Congress refused, until recently, to legislate this possible educational equality into being, the Federal Courts attempted to accomplish the task via the process of forced integration through busing. The plan was destined to fail from the beginning because it simply forced caring parents who could afford it to enroll their children in private schools or to leave the area where integration had been mandated.

"Seen in its proper perspective, education presented by well-trained, highly motivated teachers in well-designed facilities using the latest educational tools and equipment is vital to America's future; and this objective cannot be left for accomplishment to school districts that have available such vastly varied educational budgets.

"By and large, educational inequality is an economic problem rather than a racial problem. It will cease being either as citizens grasp the opportunity provided by their increased wealth and availability of reasonable mortgage money to relocate to places where adequate housing and educational facilities are available.

"To further encourage a revitalization of America's educational system, national educational standards will be established and adhered to. With excellence reestablished as a goal throughout the educational system, good teachers and administrators will be motivated to return to this vital vocation.

"In collaboration with the new Office of Corporate Conduct, companies of all sizes will be encouraged to expand on-job training for those students who choose not to seek college degrees.

"In addition to creating and sponsoring sound medical and educational programs, the Department of Humanics must advance and support cultural and recreational outlets for the citizenry.

"Remember, the overall purpose of this plan is to create a society of well-rounded, healthy human beings—physically, mentally, emotionally, and financially. Complete fulfillment of this goal requires that funding be provided to support music, drama, and art programs in addition to a wide variety of indoor and outdoor recreational programs and facilities.

"As social pressures are lessened within the newly revitalized country, similar pressures will also decrease throughout the world. To further ease world tensions simply through the process of co-mingling, increased attention will be focused on international travel. The Department of Humanics will do everything possible to aid and encourage travel by Americans.

"The Justice Department will constitute the judicial, legal, and law enforcement arm of the newly reorganized government.

"A sufficient quantity of jurists will be located in each Central Service Area to consider questions of law. To the degree possible, though, cases will be heard by a single judge. In serious criminal cases, verdicts will be handed down by a jury of five. Disputes and appeals will be heard by a panel of five jurists located at each regional capital.

"It will not be the intent that the Justice Department be authorized to declare policy decisions, issue task instructions, or create laws whether valid or invalid. This responsibility will be vested where it always should have been—in the citizenry. Each January all citizens eighteen and over will be asked to review the various acts of the Board from the previous year and express approval or disapproval via two-way television. Programs found acceptable will be left in force but reexamined every three years and then either be revalidated or discontinued.

"The Justice Department will also provide law enforcement and penal services.

"Once again, I am certain that reductions in social stress will cause a commensurate reduction in crime. But laws that are broken should entail uniform punishment of the lawbreaker. Youth, at least those above the age of responsibility, must be made to pay the price of their criminal acts. Criminal acts are equally as harmful when performed by a thirty-year-old as they are by a twelve-year-old.

"As a component of a program to reduce violent crimes in America, I propose a sharp reduction in sales of all handgun ammunition. In fact, ammunition will be made available only to legally authorized law enforcement bodies or to those personnel enrolled in officially recognized gun clubs. Those wishing to possess guns as a hobby or for sporting reasons should be permitted to do so, but fireable handguns must be taken out of the hands of those who would employ them under conditions dictated by either desperate need or strong emotion. Nearly two persons per hour are killed with handguns in America, and far too many of these are killed in moments of passion by friends, neighbors, or relatives, who, if denied the use of a loaded handgun, would have shortly returned to a state of emotional stability. The argument that 'guns don't kill, people do' must be countered with the more accurate 'mentally disturbed people using handguns kill.'

"All persons imprisoned for less than capital offenses will be given the opportunity to work at, and be paid for, constructive projects outside of the penal institutions. New America is unwilling to permit the energies of three hundred and fifty thousand inmates to be squandered in prison yard activities.

"Internationally controlled criminal organizations will be actively pursued and eliminated. In any case, much of this illegal activity will be uncovered as each person proves citizenship and each organization is chartered prior to transition day.

"In keeping with the requirements of the new low-stress society, every attempt will be made to minimize the military perception of law enforcement personnel. I am aware that previous attempts at demilitarizing law enforcement have failed; but those attempts were made against a tide of increased crime resulting from increased social stress.

"The Office of World Affairs is not simply to be a replica of the current State Department. Plans and directives sent to this department by the National Board are to concentrate on improving the lots of lesser-developed countries and our relations with them.

"Every effort is to be made to encourage countries receiving American-based corporate funds to build schools, hospitals, and infrastructure. Further, this department will be authorized to extend every effort to provide much-needed administrative know-how for any developing nation requesting it.

"We should accept the fact that these efforts will not be made solely in the spirit of magnanimity but that only through such programs are strong future trading partners developed.

"The Office of World Affairs will also manage the International Monetary Fund. The IMF will continue to perform the activities currently associated with it but, in addition, will assume the duties previously performed by the World Bank. Care is to be taken that terms of long-term, low-interest loans are to be structured to aid, rather than hinder, development of requesting governments. In the past, repayment schedules and monetary disciplines attached to such loans frequently turned out to be disastrous to the new struggling economies of the third world.

"Every policy and directive of this department is to have

as its principal aim the lowering of international tensions. The nation must cease attempting to control the world by creating competitive spheres of influence. A revitalized America will get its share of a greatly improved international marketplace.

"Current international disarmament and arms control talks must be stepped up. The continuation of spending in excess of a billion dollars a day by the superpowers for improved human extermination techniques is unconscionable.

"This lowering of dependence upon weapons must be extended to include bans on weapon sales to other countries. Time after time weapon sales made under the guise of defense have ended up being used offensively by neighboring countries.

"America's aim must be to encourage neighbors to cooperate with one another—not fight one another. The nation must abandon participating in the oft-used solution of dividing naturally cohesive countries and territories as a method of decreasing warmaking capabilities. This 'solution' has totally failed in countries such as Korea, Vietnam, or Germany.

"Finally, we come to the tenth and last of the federal offices, the Department of Defense. This department will perform many of the duties presently assigned to its current counterpart—but, with a significant change in emphasis.

"It will: maintain necessary military defense forces, procure and maintain necessary military defense equipment, and authorize and coordinate research and development programs with the Department of Technology to develop future necessary military defense equipment. The repeated use of the two words 'necessary' and 'defense' are intentional—no additional comment should be necessary.

"An example of a research and development program that fits our renewed emphasis on defense is the laser and particle-ray program—designed to knock out enemy missiles while still in outer space. A total commitment to this project, as recently requested by President Reagan, in conjunction with the recently launched Shuttle Program, could radically change the course of man's propensity to make war!"

11

Policy to Implementation

"The description of the national departments and their initial authorized tasks is fascinating, Mr. Paine, but what makes this departmental arrangement more productive than that currently in operation?" asks David.

"The critical difference, David, lies in the interrelationship of the departments to each other and to the National Board of Directors; how authority and responsibility is delegated both vertically and horizontally.

"In the case of the current departments, the secretaries are basically removed from the policy-making stream. Instead, the executive department-heads are provided authorization and money to accomplish tasks by a frequently antagonistic branch of the government—Congress.

"But, as you can see by my charts, the Federal Department Directors and Controller sit on the National Board of Directors—the only policy-making arm of the government. The directors are therefore thoroughly involved in the creation of new programs—in addition to implementing them. At no point in the new structure are there built-in opposing forces—if the board determines that some action is required, it is quickly and efficiently implemented.

"This is a good place to reemphasize the existence of one potentially opposing force, though—the electorate. As explained earlier, the citizens will be given the opportunity to veto policies annually and to review all ongoing programs for effectivity tri-annually."

"Mr. Paine, I, too, am impressed with the scope of your plan," affirms Mary. "When you advised us at the start that the plan needed to be comprehensive, I didn't realize that you meant such a complete and thorough restructuring of the nation's political, financial, and social systems. But, before we review your program up to this point, I would like you to complete the descriptions of the various government officials and their duties—and perhaps further expand the interrelationships anticipated between the three levels of the new government."

"Agreed," nods Tom Paine. "At the top post in our new corporate democracy will be a person who will perform the dual roles of President and Chairman of the National Board of Directors. While this person will continue to hold the most prestigious job in America, much of the previous competitiveness of the job will have been removed. As President, the most highly desired characteristic will be statesmanship; as Chairman of the Board, this person will need to display a dual understanding of the art of compromise and steadfastness.

"The President will be elected by the citizenry for a single, nine-year term. Thus, the nation will receive maximum benefit from his tenure—once learning the job, he will effectively lead without concern for re-election. The only other prerequisites for the person who takes the post will be that he or she be a registered citizen.

"The National Board of Directors will be made up of eighteen Directors: the heads of the ten national departments just outlined, six Regional Directors, and two Directors-at-Large. All will be elected for six-year terms—half elected each three years. One of the Directors-at-Large will be the previous President, and the other will be the principle opposition candidate in the previous election. The obvious intent of these two positions is to provide administrative continuity and to provide access to the strongest political minds available.

"Before moving on to the Regional Centers, it is appropriate to mention the fate of the numerous agencies presently in operation. During the two-year transition period leading to activation of the new government, each agency will be carefully reviewed for need. Those that have outlived their usefulness will be eliminated. Those found necessary in the new scheme of things will be assigned a useful roll in connection with one of the ten federal departments. I suspect that some of the essential duties of the regulatory agencies will be simply absorbed by an appropriate federal department. A few, such as the postal department, will likely be sold to private interests.

"I can't resist singling out one highly controversial agency for special comment—the Central Intelligence Agency. The CIA is both an asset and a liability to the current government. Unquestionably, modern governments or, for that matter, anyone operating outside the country, is in need of information regarding the idiosyncracies of non-Americans. Some of this information can even be vital to the nation's defense posture. And, to the degree that the CIA limits its activities to data gathering, it is an asset. But, at some point, this agency was permitted, if not directed, to interfere directly with the political make-up of other countries. In keeping with our planned goal of decreasing international stress, this intergovernmental interference will be suspended by this and all other agencies of the new government.

"Now, the Regional Centers are designed to represent a wider or broader segment of American society. As one level in a corporate structure, it eliminates the adversary role that many of the current states play in their relations with the federal government. Citizens must be encouraged to think nationally and parochially as citizens of local and federal governments. Up and down the corporate government structure, only one motivation must exist—servicing the needs of all American citizens.

"In keeping with this philosophy, there will be only one level of taxation. In fact, there will be only one principle tax; and, though it will be physically collected at the regional level for efficiency reasons, it will nonetheless be used to satisfy the needs of all the citizenry throughout the country. Significant cost savings will doubtless result from the elimination of the multiple and overlapping taxes previously collected at local, state, and federal levels.

"Each of the Central Service Areas will have a council consisting of twelve elected representatives. The CSA Council will, considering regional peculiarities, determine how to best inaugurate and implement policies and programs dictated by the National Board of Directors.

"In practice, then, policy or program directives emanating from the National Board of Directors will be directed to all of the affected Central Service Areas. Area and regional problems, and cost relating to implementation, will be considered and resolved by Council action and assigned to one or more of the operational departments located in the Central Service Areas for implementation.

"Thus, the Task Implementation System is designed to permit a smooth flow of information and requirements both up and down the organizational ladder. It is, as noted earlier, this ability to expeditiously and efficiently accomplish tasks, that is the hallmark and strength of the modern corporation."

12

Questions and Answers

"Well, Mr. Paine, now that we've heard your prescription for a new society, do you mind if David and I take this opportunity to ask questions as they come to mind? Hopefully, through this process we can further expand and validate your comprehensive master plan."

"No Mary, I'm delighted to accept the challenge," smiles Tom Paine—but with a renewed look of determination. "What's the first question?"

"You explained that your plan would eliminate all taxes presently being assessed at all levels and replace them with one major and two minor taxes. The major one was thoroughly defined as your Variable Instantly-applied Transaction Tax; but I don't remember you discussing the two minor taxes."

"You could have easily missed them," explains Tom Paine, "because I didn't specifically describe them as taxes—and for a reason. Both will be payments exacted from global corporations as costs of doing business away from home: one, a fifty-fifty sharing of profits with the host government, and two, a compensatory payment to the Central Service Area abandoned by a roving company. I believe both levies to be just and fair and, though obviously intended as constraints to arbitrary globe-trotting, should not be unduly restrictive or financially debilitating—remember, no other business tax is being assessed."

"That was going to be my next question," quickly responds Mary. "Do you really believe business should escape paying its fair share of the tax load in America?"

"To a number of contemporary economists and social planners, including myself, Mary, there is only one logical and fair form of taxation—one levied on consumption. All others tend to work exactly opposite to the social goal intended: property taxes discouraging buying and maintenance of homes, for example. Once this premise is understood, various taxes assessed against business are not only accepted as social evils, but are understood to be redundant as well—presently, they are simply treated as business costs and passed on to the consumer. Adam Smith recognized the relative importance of this subject when he wrote in *Wealth of Nations,* 'Consumption is the sole end and purpose of production. The time is long overdue when America accepts this fact and assesses the proper end of the production/consumption cycle for essential taxation.'

"In addition, most corporations relieved of tax payments will put the money to use as much-needed plant and equipment, plus the benefits derived from employee ownership, and should see a marked improvement in productivity. In turn, prices of goods and services will drop, further encouraging increased purchasing and ultimately lower VIT tax rates."

"Neat!" applauds David. "Now, Mr. Paine, do you think our newly emancipated citizens will accept the part of your plan that would require them to use a universal identification card?"

"Admittedly, it may take some motivational selling, but most will quickly realize and accept the many benefits available from their Lifetime Identification and Finance card. In addition to its being the key to their Personal Capital Account and the myriad of financial aids to be found there, the microprocessor LIF card will be the lifetime key to the individual's registration and voting rights, contain up-to-date micro-data of personal medical history, plus substitute for all the various identification and regulatory cards presently required—such as driver's license, age verification, and Social Security cards. To assure that the LIF card properly represents only the owner, the card will be reissued often and contain a current voice print for identification."

"But, Mr. Paine, won't the LIF card become confused with all the other credit cards carried these days?"

"No, Mary," emphasizes Tom Paine, "because the other credit and ID cards will be eliminated. To appreciate the reason for this action you have to again go back to our earlier discussions and the definition of inflation. You'll recall that this monetary problem emanated from uncontrolled increases in both money *and* credit. As you know, there are numerous forms of credit currently available; but, one of the most uncontrollable, and thus necessarily expendable, is consumer credit issued to cover credit card purchases. Gratifyingly, the use of the LIF card will provide increased convenience without the added danger of increasing inflation through capricious increases in the volume of credit.

"As an aside, let me again emphasize that low-interest, long-term loans will be available; and, I might add, with considerably less time and bother assessed to the borrower; the potential borrower's Personal Capital Account will perpetually contain all the information needed for near-instant loan evaluation.

"This is a good place to point out that the regular use of the LIF card will also, if desired, authorize payment of monthly bills from the individual's Personal Capital Account. Indeed, the number of additional timesaving financial services possible in the future is virtually unlimited. Okay, next question."

"What answer will you have, Mr. Paine, for those critics who are bound to claim that the million dollar limitation on personal wealth will stifle individual initiative and ingenuity?" asks David.

"First of all, David, in the new stable economy we're discussing, it will take considerably longer to arrive at this limit. Thus, the present quantity of six hundred thousand or so American millionaires will remain relatively static. The million dollar number, therefore, will continue to be a viable goal for most for many years to come. Secondly, the relative value or purchasing power of the million dollars will be at least four to one when compared to current values. And finally, wealthy individuals will be encouraged to form family or group corporations that would combine the net worths of many individuals. As I said earlier, it is not the intent of the plan to eliminate mansions or yachts—or the possibility of acquiring them—only to assure wider sharing of them."

"I'm not sure I understand how one million dollars obtains the equivalency of four million dollars," Mary quizzically interjects.

"Well, I'm speaking in terms of relative purchasing power," responds Tom Paine. "As the danger of double-digit inflation is eliminated, as productivity is dramatically improved, as taxation is sharply cut; and as the many other monetary improvements explained earlier take effect, the purchasing power of the dollar should easily quadruple."

"I see," nods Mary. "Let me ask you this, then. I once read that equitable taxing of income that is derived from gambling, oil, and religion would virtually eliminate the need for all other forms of taxation. It would appear that your plan lets all three of these areas off scott-free."

"Unquestionably, Mary, a considerable portion of the income from these three areas presently escapes the scrutiny of the tax collector—and each for different reasons. First, gambling is largely controlled by organized crime, and these organizations manage, through clever and devious accounting procedures, to skim off billions of unreported dollars. The giant oil companies also have learned to manipulate accounting records so that the figures maximize their profits. And few would argue convincingly that all of the billions of dollars-worth of commercial property owned by various religious organizations in America is essential to the worship of God. All of the organizations involved in these three activities will, however, be required to incorporate, and thus declare the true value of all of their property. Those who become stockholders, and this includes church members and clergy, will necessarily declare their stock value as part of their net worth. And, of course, subsequent purchases by those individuals that utilize income received as dividends, will be taxed, just as they should have been all along."

"Oh, there is the possibility that an individual might be a stockholder in more than one corporation?" suggests David.

"Oh, yes, not only the possibility but the near certainty," confirms Tom Paine. "Remember, the corporate concept is to be applied wherever there is business activity. So, it is likely that individuals will simultaneously be stockholders in several corporations; including, perhaps, a family/group corporation and a religious corporation—in addition to the corporation that is the person's principal source of income, of course."

"Mr. Paine, how does your plan treat the subject of inheritance?" continues Mary with the quiz.

"The plan wouldn't do anything to interfere with a person's right to pass wealth on to a spouse or children at the time of death. The inherited amount would be added to the heir's net worth statement, of course, and only to the degree that this might increase the total net worth beyond the million dollar limit, would inheritance be affected."

"As you know, Mr. Paine, there has been a significant increase in the amount of foreign investment in the United States in recent years. Would you alter this situation? And if so, how?" asks David.

"Well, David, as far as an overall principle is concerned, I strongly believe that America—its land and its resources, both natural and man-made—belongs to its citizens. Therefore, all foreign holdings, whether land or buildings, must be repurchased. Foreign lease arrangements and investment in commerical bonds will be encouraged, however."

It's apparent that Tom Paine is enjoying Mary's and David's strong cross-examination of his program. He feels quite confident that he has so thoroughly thought out the many varied aspects of his program that it is unlikely he can be stumped by a question.

"Another question relating to foreign involvement, Mr. Paine," resumes Mary. "Most recent Americans have been raised to believe in the invitation contained in Emma Lazurus's quote that appears as the inscription on the Statue of Liberty:

Give me your tired, your poor,
Your huddled masses yearning to breathe free,
The wretched refuse of your teeming shore,
Send these, the homeless, tempest-tossed, to me:
I lift my lamp beside the golden door.

Considering your oft-expressed concern for the current citizenry and their rights, would you now close the 'Golden door' to further immigration?"

"Another profound question, Mary; a question that can't be answered by an insensitive, simple yes or no. The history of immigration policy in America is one fraught with many inconsistencies but which, on balance, has still been generous. While it is true there are muted demands to 'take care of Americans first,' concurrently, hundreds of thousands of 'boat people' from southeast Asia and Cuba have found the arms of America still outstretched to receive them.

"I doubt if there is any historian worthy of the name who wouldn't agree that the millions who have found their way to the new world over the last two centuries added much more to the nation's rich heritage than they cost.

"However, in recent years the trickle of illegal aliens has turned into a torrent of humanity—inviting mistreatment and abuse. Thus it is that my national identification program previously outlined, is truly in the best interests of all future immigrants. Once all legal citizens are known and provided with Lifetime Identification and Finance (LIF) cards, all others will quickly become visible. All non-citizens should then be given a top priority on a first-come-first-served immigration list.

"This is a good place," continues Tom Paine, "to point out that I feel confident that, as the success of my plan becomes evident, both Canada and Mexico will desire to join an American Continental Nation; I believe such a union would be good for all parties."

"Yes, I agree with you, Mr. Paine. A strong case can be made for making the North American continent into a unified country. Each of the countries presently possesses a store of varied and unique raw materials that, if combined, would strengthen the new federated group."

"Mr. Paine, your plan would reestablish gold as backing for the dollar. How much of this scarce material does the nation possess and would you prevent the current inventory from being sold off?" asks Mary.

"Yes, I believe it is imperative that America retain its present two hundred and eighty-four million ounces of gold as collateral for its monetary system. Even at today's highly inflated values, this gold stock is worth only about a hundred billion dollars. It simply should not be permitted to further seep away, " emphasizes Tom Paine.

"One more question, Mr. Paine. Since the advent of Ronald Reagan to the political scene, we've heard more and more about 'supply-side economics.' Is this a new economic philosophy or just a new name for what we've been discussing all along?"

"No, David, 'supply-side economics' isn't new. In fact, it's just one side of the economic equation we've been talking about. It simply is a change in emphasis away from the Keynesian monetary theory, which held that economic stability could be achieved by manipulating the supply of money and credit.

"The new emphasis is on doing whatever is necessary to increase the quantity of goods and services in the marketplace. We've covered most of the actions that can influence this supply, but let's list them again: increase productivity, incentivize investment, decrease government spending, lower taxes—especially those assessed on business activities—decrease government regulations and controls on business, and eliminate government waste and corruption.

"As we've already concluded, the only plan that will now work must be comprehensive. It's just too late to cure America's economic ills by any mode short of major surgery, and this entails revising the structure of government so that it is sensitive to, and capable of reacting to, changes in both sides of the economic equation—monetary and supply."

"I have one final question, Mr. Paine. At one point in our discussion you mentioned the numerous divergent groups in America—groups with highly emotional causes such as pro-life, pro-prayer, and anti-gun. How do you think their problems will be resolved?"

"First, Mary, I believe that such divisive issues should be confronted promptly and not be permitted to simply stew in the pot. A strong administrator in the new corporate democracy will assess the various solutions and quickly put each issue to rest.

"For example, the question of whether to allow abortions might be resolved by offering a compromise that partially recognizes both pro and con positions. Few pro-abortionists would fail to agree that aborting a pregnancy in its later stages— six, seven or eight months into term, say—without medical justification is wrong. On the other hand, few pro-lifers would be terribly upset if an abortion were performed immediately upon discovery of the pregnancy—say, in the first half dozen weeks or so after conception. What this suggests, then, is that there is a reasonable solution to the dilemma: the establishment of a scientific cut-off—detection of first heartbeat or first brain activity, for example. Prior to this point an abortion would be permitted if agreed to and paid for by both the male and female partners. Beyond this point, of course, the pregnancy would necessarily be permitted to extend to full term.

"The question of whether to allow prayer in schools is complicated by the fact that it violates a basic tenet of sound democratic government: the separation of church and state. Frankly, I don't believe a law should be written nor a court ruling made concerning this subject. My preference would be to encourage school administrators to provide appropriate times during the school day for religious students of all faiths to make silent prayers.

"I earlier expressed my strong opposition to current handgun possession laws. Unquestionably, handguns are involved in unnecessary deaths. My solution, as stated earlier, would avoid the highly emotional subject of registration or confiscation of handguns: diligent control of the sale of ammunition and ammunition materials. This method solves the problem over a period of years as unnecessary users exhaust their ammunition supplies. It should be noted that a few communities in the U.S. are starting to employ the more direct approach of passing ordinances that make it illegal to own or possess handguns. This problem has become so critical that any solution that works is welcome," concludes Tom Paine.

"I too have one final question, Mr. Paine. I noticed that you used the descriptive phrase 'nationally-owed' when stating your intent to cancel the current federal debt. Are you implying that the foreign-owned portion of the debt would be honored?"

"Yes, David. Americans traditionally have held their credit-worthiness in high esteem. And though they might choose to eliminate that portion of the debt owed to themselves when they consider the sizeable bonus to be received, they probably would insist on honoring the fifteen percent or so of the debt owed to outsiders who will not otherwise be compensated."

13

Assignment Resolution and Tomorrow

"Mr. Paine, unless David has additional questions at this time, I'd like to suggest that we review your plan from the top to see if it resolves all of the problems we detailed in our original assignment."

"Good, Mary. David, why don't you lead off with a review of the number one nemesis, inflation."

"All right Mr. Paine. Let me see." David stands thoughtfully for a moment while mentally reconstructing the earlier lessons: "You started the discussion of inflation by pointing out how it was directly or indirectly responsible for most of the ills of the country and surprised us by revealing an exact definition and identity of the responsible parties.

"The definition clearly suggested," continues David, "that positive control over the growth of money and credit would be necessary if inflation is to be stopped. And your discussion relating to the identity of the responsible parties clearly placed the blame at the doorstep of the Federal Reserve System. In addition, you argued convincingly that the integrity of the dollar as a monetary unit had to be restored.

"If I understand the resolutions of these problems contained in your plan, the following changes would be required: first, the Federal Reserve would be replaced by a new federal Controller, but without the authority to unilaterally issue money; second, credit would be severely monitored and controlled by the new Controller; third, use of other international currencies would be permitted in payment of debt; fourth, both the country's gold and its land resources would be pledged as collateral for international debt, and finally, the stock of goods and services would be automatically increased as the productivity of the workplace improved. Doesn't that about cover the subject in a nutshell?"

"Yes, very good David. Now Mary, pick up where David left off and expand on the subject of productivity."

"All right, Mr. Paine. We learned that productivity is a much more complex subject than most believe, involving changes in use and condition of plant and equipment in addition to the human variables resulting from such things as worker motivation or fatigue. We also learned that the possibility for improvement in productivity varied extensively according to whether the worker was producing goods or providing services, and that the negative by-products of productivity were often unemployment or higher taxes, rather than inflation. Your plan would assure continued improvement in productivity by requiring all businesses other than self-employed individuals, to be converted to employee-owned corporations."

"So far, my star students are earning A's," smiles Tom Paine. "Your turn, David. We spent considerable time exploring the process by which corporations quite literally exploded in size and area represented and are now challenging their base countries for supremacy. What conclusions were reached as regards my master plan?"

"Yes," responds David, "I found that discussion both enlightening and disturbing; and, I might say I was both somewhat relieved, but nonetheless startled, when you disclosed how you planned to fight fire with fire by reshaping the federal government to fit a corporate mold. As radical as this approach is, I have come to accept it as being essential to that unstable and mercurial world down there.

"I studied your Task Implementation chart very carefully, Mr. Paine, and can readily see where a small, highly homogenous group like the National Board of Directors would be able to react to virtually any kind of crisis situation much more expeditiously than the current burdensome combination of executive and legislative groups. All that would be necessary to resolve a problem, it would appear, is for the Board to define the issue, break it into one or more tasks, and assign the tasks—along with the proper funding—to one or more federal departments for implementation through the affected Central Service Areas. Any parochial peculiarities would be resolved in the Central Service Area Councils.

"I sincerely doubt," adds David, "that if such an organization had been in place in contemporary America, it would have taken years to plan and implement legislation as critical as the recently adopted national energy program."

"Good, David. I'm glad you emphasized the expedient nature of a small, efficient group like the National Board; in today's time-oriented society it is one of the most important assets. Now, Mary; can you pick up on the subject of global corporations and summarize how the plan would regulate their future activities?"

"Yes, Mr. Paine. You have outlined several constraints to the future movements of international corporations, including having them cough up payment of any costs that might accrue to the local Central Service Area as a result of relocating elsewhere.

"But perhaps the most vital discipline would evolve from the new government's insistence on accurate and current data disclosure. This would permit timely assessment and remedy of variations in import prices that are solely the result of cheap labor pools existing in some remote corner of the world.

"Oh! and I mustn't forget the fifty-percent-of-corporate-profits refund to host countries. I, personally, wouldn't be surprised if this feature of your plan might well turn out to be the most important ingredient of all," predicts Mary. "Certainly, I can't imagine any move more likely to ease international tensions."

"Thank you. It's certainly gratifying to see that both of you have apparently accepted the essence of my plan. But before we continue with a discussion of how to best implement it, let me ask you, Mary, to comment on the part that the citizenry will be asked to play in interfacing with the new government."

"All right, Mr. Paine. My mental picture of the role you've outlined would have several days, perhaps as long as a week, dedicated to reviewing the previous year's government activities. I can foresee lively debates erupting throughout the nation in the days leading up to the actual voting. And, when Government Week is over, the people, through their vote of consent or rejection, will have directly participated in shaping their own destiny—and I believe that to be the epitome of democratic ideals."

"Good, Mary. You've truly captured the spirit of my new People's Corporate Democracy. Now comes the most important question of all—what are the chances of implementing my master plan? Would either of you like to make a personal assessment?"

"Well, Mr. Paine, I think of myself as a pragmatist," offers David. "So, until recently I would have given virtually no chance that such a sweeping plan as yours could actually become reality. But if what I've learned from your lecture is true, there is little hope for significant continued improvement in the economy as a result of programs offered by either national political party; indeed, there is strong evidence that the economy will again worsen in the near future."

"Yes, I agree, David. The 1980 election, which saw the Republicans win the Presidency and Senate, has been interpreted as a major shift towards conservative government; but, in fact, the electorate was only casting around for someone or something that might turn the country around. The American people, in spite of their current problems, are pragmatic, sensitive, and logical, over the long haul, when dealing with their own fate.

"In the first year following his election, President Reagan was successful in getting Congress to enact laws which would lower taxes, cut spending in some areas, and reduce regulatory abuses on business.

"The Federal Reserve, in the meantime, under the continued direction of Chairman Paul Volcker, has continued to allow monetary growth to gyrate wildly while encouraging interest rates to remain unnaturally high. This course of action has kept the economy hee-hawing back and forth while endorsing foreign-dollar investment that in turn has helped to excessively strengthen the exchange value of the dollar as compared with the other ten principle world currencies.

"Then a somewhat unexpected thing happened: inflation fell almost ten percentage points! Why? Because the high value of the dollar made imports relatively cheap, and thus foreign goods flowed into the U.S. in huge volume—the imbalance of trade in '83 nearing the $100 billion mark, in fact.

"Note how the marketplace has become international as a result: the supply side of our old inflation equation is filled, not only by American goods and services, but by world-wide goods and services. Thus, even during the recent recessions, when America was naturally constraining its output, the void in demand was continually filled with foreign goods. Needless to say, this occurrence, though having the positive outcome of lowering inflation, had the negative result of keeping many millions of Americans unemployed.

"Of course, the point of all of this is to illustrate the need for change—not just an adjustment here and there, but a total overhaul that will help stabilize the daily lives of all 235 million Americans.

"Unless something akin to the program we've outlined is adopted, a severe danger exists that the current problems will continue to grow ever worse until inevitably our friends are threatened with first economic and then military disaster."

"Oh, dear God, stop, Mr. Paine!" cries Mary. "Must our beloved America be taken to the brink of total calamity before it willingly accepts the fact that sound, sane solutions to its problems are available?"

"No, Mary, it's not necessary that America be driven to the brink of disaster, but unfortunately, it will take shocking evidence similar to that just described before sufficient numbers of citizens awaken to the deepening peril. Only then will they take the necessary steps to avert disaster."

"But what can they do, anyway?" asks David excitedly.

"When we accepted this assignment, we each had one thing in common; a deep, unswerving devotion to America. But that devotion wasn't, or isn't, blind. By now we should be completely sensitive to America's strengths and weaknesses."

"Unquestionably, its greatest strength lies in its people: people collected from the four corners of the earth; people with wit, intelligence, imagination, determination, and courage."

"That's all well and good, Mr. Paine," Mary impatiently interrupts. "But, specifically, what can be done?"

"Believe me my young friends, I'm not underestimating the task. It will not be accomplished by the simple wave of a wand. But, fortunately, we are dealing with a most uncommon breed of men and women. They have shown unprecedented courage in the face of overwhelming odds before. In the dead of winter of 1776, I wrote:

> These are the times that try men's souls. The summer soldier and the sunshine patriot will, in this crisis, shrink from the service of his country; but he that stands it *now*, deserves the love and thanks of man and woman. Tyranny, like hell, is not easily conquered; yet we have this consolation with us, that the harder the conflict, the more glorious the triumph. What we obtain too cheap, we esteem too lightly; 'tis dearness only that gives everything its value. Heaven knows how to put a proper price upon its goods; and it would be strange indeed, if so celestial an article as *Freedom* should not be highly rated.

"With my pen outlining the way, my earlier compatriots proved that they were neither summer soldiers nor sunshine patriots; they did not shrink from their duty: to themselves, to their families, to their country.

"They met and subdued the overseas enemy, met and founded a democratic republic where, they hoped, freedom and equality would be responsibly balanced, met and conceived an economic and social environment in which to nurture their natural instincts for pride, dignity, and self-respect.

"Now, two centuries later, unpredictable events and forces have created new and even more urgent demands."

"Mr. Paine, I believe your plan can meet these new, urgent demands. But how can that plan be implemented?" insists Mary.

"Well, if you'll recall, Mary, you interrupted my description of tomorrow's scenario at the point at which things were potentially going from bad to worse throughout America. And, if not for one vitally important characteristic of America, the problems might grow to unsolvable proportions. The characteristic I refer to is that America is still a democracy—and thus, Americans still hold their ultimate destiny—for better or worse—in their own hands.

"They have been given the gift of the gods: they possess within them, individually and collectively, the power to create their life in whatever form they choose. Without fully understanding it, they have this power, this eternal force that has come to be known as the American spirit—that indomitable will to create a better world for themselves and their posterity. And so it will be that our threatened and badly jostled friends will assess their peril and rise up and demand a new, responsive government.

"As we near the celebration of our Constitution's 200th year, more and more perceptive Americans are aware that the current model is not working well. So I foresee that, early in the next decade, the American people will assess their future needs and demand a constitutional convention. After much deliberation, the convention will produce a *new* constitution that *starts* with a Citizen's Bill of Rights *and* Responsibilities and goes on to formulate a new government—similar to our recently devised people's corporate democracy.

"Something like a two-year transitional period will be necessary while the new government is formed and the economic measures contained in our plan readied for implementation. Then comes the momentous transition day: a new, lean, responsive government goes to work for the people. As confidence is restored and stresses abate, the economic structure stabilizes and the social institutions return to normal. Crime quickly diminishes, unemployment drops, and a fair and equitable distribution of wealth becomes available to all.

"Instead of 'these are the times that try men's souls,' I will proclaim 'these are the times that fill men's souls with hope and joy!' "

Epilogue

And there you have it! Tom Paine's original, provocative, and promising new approach to government. I, for one, salute him and pledge to work diligently toward the fulfillment of his goal.

But how about you, dear reader, are you ready to dismiss the book as just another doomsday epoch—that ever-present apocalypse of man's downfall? Or are you ready to concede that it is, instead, a vitally important formula for how America can resolve its current dilemma—hopefully, in time to adjust to a future of peaceful, harmonious living?

Has our recent mentor provided a sufficiently detailed historical backdrop from which to evaluate the causes of today's debacle? How, you might astutely ask, would corporate democracy fare when pitted against its three strongest contemporary political/economic competitors: socialism, communism, despotism? Is it not true that these systems as they have finally evolved, are designed to sublimate, dominate, or subjugate all to the unresponsive social mass, insensitive political state, or self-indulgent despot? Is it not also true that this new-model democracy represents the antithesis of these tried and failed 'isms? Indeed, this system is capable of raising the individual to the ultimate lofty plane where government acts as man's civil servant, not his overlord.

What of Tom Paine's emphasis upon the redistribution of land and wealth? And does the plan achieve an equitable balance between freedom and equality without constraining man's natural instinct for pride, dignity, and self-respect in his ever-present quest for self-improvement?

A friend, responding to my request to read and critique an early draft of this book, was outspoken in his belief that there were too many powerful opposing forces for the plan to become reality. But if this new government concept represents the path to a vastly improved way of life—as I believe it does—it must ultimately become reality in spite of these seemingly overwhelming obstacles. Inherent in this belief is the unacceptability of the various alternative paths and in the certainty that man does possess both the ability and motivation to fulfill his destiny.

The bottom-line question is, can we who believe in the viability of Tom Paine's corporate democracy do anything personally to help bring it to fruition? The answer is a resounding "yes"! Do just one small act: talk to your friends and convince just one that the plan is the answer. If he convinces another, and so on, the concept will sweep the country like a giant prairie fire.

* * *

> Society in every state is a blessing, but Government, even in its best state, is but a necessary evil; in its worst state, an intolerable one.
>
> *Thomas Paine, 1776*

Bibliography

Barnet, Richard J., and Muller, Ronald E. *Global Reach: The Power of the Multinational Corporation.* New York: Simon & Schuster, 1974.

Bell, Daniel. *The Cultural Contradictions of Capitalism.* New York: Basic Books, 1976

Bellamy, Edward. *Looking Backward.* New York: New American Library, 1960.

———. *Equality.* New York: AMS Press, 1970.

Bladen, Ashby. *How to Cope With the Developing Financial Crisis.* New York: McGraw-Hill, 1980.

Boorstin, Daniel J. *The Republic of Technology.* New York: Harper & Row, 1978.

Bronowski, J. *The Ascent of Man.* Boston, Massachusetts: Little, Brown & Co., 1973.

Carnoy, Martin, and Shearer, Derek. *Economic Democracy: The Challenge of the 1980s.* White Plains, New York: M.E. Sharpe, 1980.

Churchman, C.A. *The Systems Approach.* New York: Delacorte Press, 1968.

Current, Richard N., Williams, Harry T., and Freidel, Frank. *American History: A Survey.* New York: Alfred A. Knopf, 1961.

Curtis, Michael. *The Great Political Theories, Volumes 1 & 2.* New York: Avon, 1961.

Drucker, Peter F. *Men, Ideas & Politics.* New York: Harper & Row, 1971.

Ebenstein, William. *Great Political Thinkers: Plato to the Present.* Hinsdale, Illinois: Dryden Press, 1969.

Edmunds, Stahrl W. *Alternative U.S. Futures.* Santa Monica, California: Goodyear Publishing Co., 1978.

Friedman, Milton. *Capitalism and Freedom.* Chicago, Illinois: University of Chicago Press, 1962.

Frisch, Robert A. *The Magic of ESOT: The Fabulous New Instrument of Corporate Finance.* Rockville Center, New York: Farnsworth Publishing, 1975.

Galbraith, John Kenneth. *The Age of Uncertainty.* Boston, Massachusetts: Houghton Mifflin Co., 1977.

Gill, Richard T. *Economics and the Public Interest.* Pacific Palisades, California: Goodyear Publishing Co., 1968.

Grant, Sir Alexander. *Aristotle.* Edinburgh, England: Folcroft Library Editions, 1977.

Hazlitt, Henry. *The Inflation Crisis, and How to Resolve it.* New Rochelle, New York: Arlington House Publishers, 1978.

Heilbroner, Robert L. *The Worldly Philosophers: The Lives, Times, and Ideas of the Great Economic Thinkers.* New York: Simon & Schuster, 1967.

Henderson, Hazel. *Creating Alternative Futures: The End of Economics.* New York: Berkley Publishing Corp., 1978.

Kahn, Herman, with the Hudson Institute. *World Economic Development—1979 and Beyond.* New York: Morrow Quill, 1979.

Lamb, Edward. *The Sharing Society.* Seacaucus, New Jersey: Lyle Stuart, Inc., 1979.

Lasch, Christopher. *The Culture of Narcissism: American Life in an Age of Diminishing Expectations.* New York: W.W. Norton, 1979.

Magdoff, Harry. *The Age of Imperialism: The Economics of U.S. Foreign Policy.* New York: Monthly Review Press, 1969.

Miliband, Ralph. *The State in Capitalist Society.* New York: Basic Books, Inc., 1969.

Morgan, Arthur E. *Nowhere Was Somewhere: How History Makes Utopias and How Utopias Make History.* New York: Van Rees Press, 1946.

———. *The Philosophy of Edward Bellamy.* New York: King's Crown Press, 1945.

Myrdal, Alva. *The Game of Disarmament: How the United States & Russia Run the Arms Race.* New York: Pantheon, 1976.

Naibitt, John. *Megatrends.* New York: Warner Books, Inc., 1984 (Updated Edition).

Paine, Thomas. Introduction to *Common Sense,* by Kramnick, Isaac. Middlesex, England: Penguin Books, 1976.

———. Introduction to *Rights of Man,* by Collins, Henry. Middlesex, England: Penguin Books, 1976.

Panofsky, W.K.H. *Arms Control and SALT II.* Seattle, Wash.: University of Washington Press, 1979.

Rimmer, Robert H. *Love Me Tomorrow.* New York: New American Library, 1978.

Roberts, Jane. *Psychic Politics.* Englewood Cliffs, New Jersey: Prentice-Hall, 1976.

———. *The Nature of Personal Reality.* Englewood Cliffs, N.J.: Prentice-Hall, 1974.

Roszak, Theodore. *Person/Planet: The Creative Disintegration of Industrial Society.* Garden City, N.Y.: Anchor Press-Doubleday, 1979.

Rothbard, Murray N. *For a New Liberty; The Libertarian Manifesto.* New York: Macmillan Publishing, 1973.

Sabine, George H. *A History of Political Theory—Fourth Edition.* Hinsdale, Ill.: Dryden Press, 1973.

Schumacher, E.F. *Small Is Beautiful: Economics As If People Mattered.* New York: Harper & Row, 1973.

Shuman, James B. and Rosenau, David. *The Kondratieff Wave: The Future of America Until 1984 and Beyond.* New York: Dell Publishing, 1972.

Smith, Adam, Introduction by Skinner, Andrew. *The Wealth of Nations.* Middlesex, England: Penguin Books, 1970.

Smith, Edward Conrad, ed. *The Constitution of the United States: With Case Summaries.* New York: Harper & Row, 1972.

Stavrianos, L.S. *The Promise of the Coming Dark Age.* San Francisco: W.H. Freeman & Co., 1976.

Thompson, William Irwin. *At the Edge of History.* New York: Harper Torchbooks, 1971.

Toffler, Alvin. *The Eco-spasm Report.* New York: Bantam, 1975.

Wattenberg, Ben J. *In Search of the Real America.* New York: Doubleday, 1978.

Wanniski, Jude. *The Way the World Works.* New York: Simon & Schuster, 1978.

Wilson, James Q. *Thinking About Crime.* New York: Random House, 1977.

National Planning Association—Center for Economic Projections. *Basic Maps of the U.S. Economy 1967–1990: Population, Employment, & Income.* Washington, D.C., Dec. 1979.

U.S. Department of Agriculture—Economics, Statistics & Cooperatives Service, *Who Owns the Land: A Preliminary Report of a U.S. Landownership Survey (ESCS 70).* Washington, D.C., Sept. 1979.

Index